Real Estate Advertising That *Works!*

Real Estate Advertising That *Works!*

Linda Lipman

ARGYLE PRESS, INC.

6312 Santa Ana Canyon • Suite 193 • Anaheim • California • 92807

ALSO AVAILABLE FROM ARGYLE PRESS

Successful Farming—By Mail
Successful Farming—By Phone
2,001 Winning Ads for Real Estate

Cataloging in Publication Data

Lipman, Linda
    Real estate advertising that works!

    (Real estate for professional practitioners)
    Includes index.

ISBN 0-944041-05-1

Printed in the United States of America.

Contents

1.
Ideas to Get You Started

Before you start advertising yourself, your company or your listings, it's a good idea to spend some time doing your homework. You know how much it helps to preview listings before you show a home to a prospective buyer. You know that you must keep abreast of all the available financing options. You know that you must prepare a presentation before a listing appointment. In other words, if you don't plan for your clients — or do your homework — you won't have much of a chance of closing a transaction and collecting a commission.

The same type of preparation is just as necessary and even more crucial in advertising. If you haven't prepared for showing a prospect some appropriate homes, you won't actually lose money. But if you advertise haphazardly, it will cost you dearly. Advertising is expensive — one of the largest controllable costs you face each month. Bad advertising will not only cost you in expenses for ad production and space but also in lost phone calls and sales It might turn off your potential clients before they can decide to do business with you.

The old theory that all advertising pays off in some way really isn't true. Bad advertising is expensive. But you can't place or pay for enough good advertising.

This chapter has been designed to give you a quick overview of the major areas you need to consider and the key decisions you need to make in order to create an effective advertising strategy. We'll begin by discussing how you can define your personal and company images and show you how you can communicate those images effectively through your advertising.

Your Image

Before deciding what your company image and/or your personal image is, sit down and analyze why a property seller or buyer should use your services instead of a competitor's. If you don't know why, start asking some of your recent clients why they chose your firm and what they particularly liked about doing business with you.

If you're a new broker or sales associate, decide how your image will fit into your market area. Should you be folksy and homespun, or sophisticated and extravagant? Should you appeal to the high-end buyer or the bargain basement shopper?

One very successful sales associate found that her image and advertising were all wrong for the blue-collar farm area she initially selected. The stylish and slim brunette was using her picture in her ads and was working the neighborhood door-to-door. She got no response. Even though her image was very attractive, it was preventing her from communicating to her farm area. She finally realized that she needed to change her farm to an area that could identify with her style and then direct her advertising to that new market.

Many very successful salespeople zero in on a particular market rather than attempting to be a jack-of-all-trades. You should know the advantages of farming a particular area for business. If your clients know that you are a specialist not only in their community but in their particular subdivision, they will believe that you can offer them better service than another broker or sales associate who works a 50-square-mile area with no specific knowledge of their neighborhood.

When you create your image, consider the benefits of positioning: choosing a narrow market like first-time home buyers, luxury home buyers or condo buyers. Then start promoting your image in relation to the positioning you have chosen. Also start selling the *benefits* of your services rather than the *features* of your qualifications in your advertising.

Think about any product that you're considering buying: a computer, for example. If a computer company ad announced that its package included "mouse, RAM card, utility guide, composite monitor, joystick, dual disk drive and 15 resident fonts," you might just turn the page. But if the ad read, "Look like a million for under $3,000" and showed a crisp typeset document next to one printed with a poor quality dot-matrix printer, you'd see the benefits of desktop publishing and a laser printer right away.

That's more important than knowing the mechanical features of the system. If you decided to buy this system, it would be because of the system's obvious benefits to you.

Also remember to stress the *benefits* of using your services as a sales associate or broker. Don't just focus on the *features* of your firm, like the relocation department, property management services or membership in a national franchise or organization. Appeal to your market's need to buy or sell. Translate your company's features into real benefits.

Building on Your Name

After you have defined your corporate image, you need to develop a way to communicate that image. Why have so many Hollywood movie stars changed the names they were born with? And why do companies research names, color combinations and styles before they design their letterheads, choose their company names and hoist the signs for their buildings?

Because your name, and expanded on that identity, your logo, will leave an image in your public's mind of what type of organization you represent. That doesn't mean that you should change your name or invest in color research. But do consider how you want your name featured in your ads so that it gives people an indelible and favorable impression of your company.

Most people prefer to do business with a company they know by name. Your logo is the quickest and most effective way to increase your name recognition among your public. People may not read all of the copy in your ads or remember what company advertised the house they saw for sale, but they just might notice your logo.

Therefore, a logo should be one of the first tools you complete for your marketing/advertising program. The sooner you have it, the sooner you can use it to build recognition. Even if you've never had a logo, you can start using one now. Once you've chosen a logo, use it regularly on all printed materials and especially in all ads.

What's a Logo?

The logo is simply a graphic device or symbol that helps communicate the name of your company and the image that you wish to convey. For example, if you want your company to be viewed as a progressive and forward-thinking organization, you might choose a geometric futuristic shape as your logo.

5

On the other hand, if you want to portray your company as a warm and caring organization, you might choose a homey or old-fashioned symbol. Since the logo is visual, it can give you an image of strength, modernism or hometown feeling. It can also communicate the product you are associated with — homes or other types of real property. *Strong visual appeal* is the key to the logo since most people notice illustrations before they read copy.

However, since one of your goals is to generate name recognition in your community, make sure that your name is part of your logo. Don't just choose some pyramid or abstract shape that you like.

In fact, you may decide to use your company name in a distinctive type style as your logo if the type makes a visual statement. One firm uses the owner's signature as its logo. By using his signature, this broker believes that he is demonstrating to the public that he stands behind what he sells.

Do some soul searching before you get started on your logo design. What do you want this mark to communicate about your company or services? Be prepared to discuss this and the following points with your graphic artist:

1. The nature of your business
2. Your customer profile
3. Your current image or the image you want to project

In evaluating logo designs, first consider how they fit in with your current needs — business card, yard signs, even classified ads. Does the logo look good when it's reduced as well as oversized? You could even take it to a printer or your newspaper's advertising department to get opinions on how it will reproduce. Here are some points you should consider in evaluating the logo design:

1. Does it need some expensive custom typesetting? Can it be used with different type and still be distinctive?

2. Is it simple, yet unique? You don't want it to look like one of your competitor's.

3. Can it last? You want the logo to have an appeal that can last for years, rather than a trendy design that will be outdated quickly.

4. Does it communicate something about your company or is it just a visual symbol?

Add a Slogan

Besides your company name and logo, you may want to incorporate a slogan or identifying line into your ads. Even salespeople now are developing and using their own logos and slogans to make their names familiar.

One San Diego broker, Jeff Shea, uses "Just Shea When." He started that slogan as a sales associate and it appears on his business card, his classifieds, his display ads, even the license plate on his car. He says some people don't even know his full name, but they know to "Just Shea When." That's all he needs.

For years, Century 21 used "National, but neighborly" to incorporate the benefits of being big with the small community-minded spirit of the local real estate agent. Then they changed to "Put number one to work for you." Most Century 21 ads now include this new slogan. Another franchise organization, Partners, uses the "Get ready to move" slogan in its ads.

You can use a slogan as part of an identity package that includes your company name and logo, or it can be a line added whenever you believe it is needed.

You also could have a variety of slogans that you use alternately, such as: "Serving Your Hometown for Over 25 Years," "Think of Us First, We'll Think of You First," "The Housing Specialists," "Over $50 Million in Sales This Year." Whatever you choose, give your slogan the same consideration you gave your logo. You want it to be short and say something beneficial about your firm.

Both the logo and slogan should stand out in your ads. Give the logo sufficient space to make a statement. You can save space costs by cramming it into an ad that is overloaded with copy, but that defeats the purpose of spending money on designing something that you're proud of.

8

Although you may have some ideas about the design of your logo, it's best to meet with a graphic designer and typesetter for the actual production. After you have told them what you want, they will present you with several prototypes to choose from. Once you have made your selection, ask the artist for several different sized "stats" (camera-ready art). You will need them for your letterhead, business card, brochures, classified ads and display ads.

Know Your Media

One of the biggest questions that real estate professionals face is where to advertise. It seems that the list of publications continues to grow daily. Some of the homework you must do before deciding where to advertise is to familiarize yourself with the available media and learn what markets they reach.

Your market and image could be correct, the benefits might be there, you may have even hired a New York ad agency to design your logo and compose a fifteen-word classified — but if you place your ad in the wrong publication, all your efforts will be wasted.

For example, the *Los Angeles Times* is a daily newspaper that claims to reach over three million people on Sundays. While this may sound impressive, your local Home Town News reaches more people in your market area who would be more likely to use your services. Placing your ads in a prestigious paper that boasts a large circulation may not always be the most effective way to advertise.

In this case, placing them in a smaller, less prestigious local newspaper may be more effective, since this paper may be a better way to reach your market area. In fact, daily newspapers are experiencing so much competition from local weeklies that many of them are starting their own weekly or daily suburban supplements to reach only the circulation that the advertiser needs, at lower rates. Studies also have shown that people often spend more time reading their local papers than they do the metropolitan dailies.

For example, Shoppers (small newspapers consisting only of classified ads that are given away free at grocery stores) used to advertise only garage sales and baby-sitters for hire.

However, they now often include listings for new car dealerships, homes valued at over $300,000 and new business opportunities. If you think people who are in the market for something as serious as a new home don't read Shoppers, you're wrong.

Some large metropolitan daily newspapers are so worried about the impact of Shoppers that they have started their own classified ad sections mailed free to all homes — not just their subscribers — in their entire circulation area. Some of these metropolitan classified sections look just like the Shoppers.

The key to effective ad placement is media research which will be discussed at length in chapter 5.

The Budget

A very important point to remember about your advertising is that most people who don't know you will judge you and your company not by its accomplishments, but by the image you project in your marketing materials.

You may have a first-class operation in every respect but if you decide to cut back on your advertising expenditures or the time spent developing well thought-out ads, people will not only think that your advertising looks second rate, they'll think that your company is second rate too, even if they've never visited your office or dealt with any of your sales associates. Therefore, to the public, your advertising *is* you.

Once you've researched the media available and are familiar with their rates, formulate a starting budget for your advertising. Otherwise your costs can get quickly out of hand. There are always more publications and editions to advertise in than any advertiser can afford, so plan on a budget and stick with it.

Decide if you're going to advertise your listings daily, weekly, bi-weekly or monthly. Are you going to advertise a higher priced property more frequently because of the increased commission the sale will generate? Should salespeople be given a budget based on the number of listings they have? Are you going to advertise just to increase your name recognition and develop your image in the community? If you are, you should remember that this kind of institutional or image advertising takes time to pay dividends, just as farming does.

Finally, how are you going to decide on an annual budget? Will it be based on net profit? Many brokers and salespeople spend between ten and twenty-five percent of their gross incomes on advertising and marketing. While your budget should be in line with your expected sales, don't eliminate your advertising completely in the slow season. That might just put you out of business. How to set an advertising budget is discussed in detail in chapter 11.

2.
Your Listings Demand It — Classified Advertising

A dvertising is one of the main ways a listing agent can prove he is fulfilling his contractual obligation "to use diligence in procuring a purchaser." Since advertising is nearly a must for every listing, most brokers and salespeople rely on the newspaper classified sections.

But classified advertising also serves other purposes. If you've been in business any length of time at all, you know that a good classified for a particular listing will make the phone ring. But the ultimate result usually isn't a sale of the property advertised. In other words, a classified for one property may result in a sale of another unadvertised listing.

You also need to advertise for another reason, even if you don't think that classifieds will

MONTVALE $242,000
BRAND NEW LISTING!
IMMACULATE
and waiting for you to move right in is this beautifully maintained 2 BedRm Townhouse. LR/fplc, formal DR, garage. All amenities and low taxes. This home is realistically priced & a "REAL FIND"

YOURNAME
REALTORS

Street Address   City
555-6789

sell your listings: your competition advertises and you need to get your name in front of the public at least as often as they do. You may even find that sellers compare listing agents based on how often they claim their listings will be advertised. If your competition says that they will advertise weekly and if you want the listing, you may have to match that offer.

Even if you would like to use display advertising exclusively (although I don't recommend it), you should still try classifieds before you incur the higher cost of display space. They are a great place to test your headline, appeal or offer.

If you find the response is good in the classified section, you can rework the same ad for the display space. If the ad hasn't been successful, you haven't invested much in classified space compared to the more expensive display position. You may also want to use the classified sections for recruitment purposes and to increase listings, the lifeblood of the real estate business.

If you understand why people read the classifieds, you'll have a better key to writing successful ads. There are three kinds of classified readers.

Why People Read Classifieds

First are "ready, willing and able" buyers — the type of shoppers you should be most interested in. Since the classified section is tucked away from the rest of the newspaper, only those who are active buyers seek out this section.

Think of it this way, a reader interested in buying furniture can turn to the classifieds and read the furniture classified ad listings rather than scouring the newspaper for any display (large) ads that run alongside the editorial space. (These ads are called ROP, or Run of Paper.) Readers not interested in furniture don't bother to read the furniture listings in the classified pages.

The second type of classified reader is lukewarm, but you should be interested in making your advertising attractive to him as well. This reader casually looks through classifieds and will act if something strikes his eye. He's interested only in something out of the ordinary or at a low price. If he finds something in one of those categories, he will call to find out the details and

15

OPEN

SUNDAY

1:30 - 4:30

510 HIGHLAND

IDEAL FAMILY HOME

Designed with ample space for family living, with 3 baths and 4 bedrooms. You will
enjoy the family room with cathedral ceiling and fireplace. Only 6 mo. old. Owner
and Builder: Frankie Newby. Priced in the
mid $130's. (510—H)

DIRECTIONS: West Old Madison Pike,
Right on Liller Blvd., Left Highland

HOSTESS: Freddie Hancock

YOURNAME

Realty   555-6789

may even make a purchase, even if he wasn't in
the market for whatever was listed in the ad.

The third type of classified reader is the
continual browser who isn't looking to buy anything. He reads classified ads for the same reason other readers are addicted to their comics
sections — leisure reading. However, this is just
the type of reader who will decide who to list his
house with based on how often he has seen your
ads in the classified section and how prominent
your ads are compared to your competitors'.
Obviously, getting noticed by this type of reader
is very important to any real estate agent who
wants to increase his listings.

Another reason people read their local

newspaper's real estate classifieds is the same reason they read the rest of their local news. They want the local news on who has their house on the market, what they're asking for it, how long it's been on the market, where the open houses are scheduled for the weekend and in general, current neighborhood home values. By reaching this type of reader, the listing agent who placed the ad is really a source of community news. And that's a position that serves to enhance his reputation.

As a real estate professional, you can realize many benefits by reading the real estate classifieds. First of all, it's a good way to keep track of all activity in your farm area, whether you're reading listings of another broker or For-Sale-By-Owners (FSBOs). You can't convert FSBOs unless you know they're out there — advertising themselves. Keep track of how long you've seen their ads, then use that information to get an appointment for a listing presentation with the seller.

To make sure that your classified ads will appeal to a certain group of classified ad readers and that your advertising dollars will not be wasted, it is important to "position" the home. That means establishing a probable market for it before you begin advertising. But before you can do this, you must familiarize yourself with the home. The best time to do this is immediately

The Listing Appoint-ment

"Young Family Needed" — gets even more specific in addressing family needs. Young families often have "immature" price budgets.

YOUNG FAMILY NEEDED

for this super 3 bedroom, 2-1/2 bath home in the hills. Great room with massive rock fireplace, large master suite, generous storage and room for expansion. Only $69,500.

FIRST LASTNAME

555-6789

YOURNAME

COMPANY   REALTORS

Street Address   Company phone

after you and the seller have completed the listing agreement.

At this point, you'll need to complete the listing sheet with all of the home's features for your buyers or the Multiple Listing Service (MLS). While this helps you to become a complete reference source on your listing, completing lengthy forms detailing how many trees are on the property, what type of tile is in the bathroom or how new the dishwasher is won't help you in writing your classified ad for the property.

Classified ads are usually too brief to mention many of the details of the listing. Those long forms listing all the features of the home may only serve to confuse you about which are the most important benefits to include in your ad.

One of the best ways to identify a probable market for a home is to ask the current owners what they particularly enjoy about living there.

OPEN HOUSE 1-4
1535 West 26th
OUR BEST BUY!!

Brand new on market, 3 bedroom, 1-3/4 bath, family room-kitchen combination, semi-formal dining room, weatherized, shake roof. Located in wonderful West Eugene foothills area. A surprise at only $52,950. Your hostess: First Lastname, 555-6789.

—Valley River Branch—

YOURNAME & YOURNAME

Street Address Realtors Company Phone

*"Our Best Buy"
— good head-
line choice for
attracting
bargain hunt-
ers — a big
category of
home buyers.*

You might be surprised to hear them say that they'll miss their neighbors or that they'll miss watching the sunsets from their patio.

These are two benefits that might easily escape the listing agent who hasn't done his homework. Friendly neighbors could be a real selling point, especially to a relocating family. As for sunsets, try finding a parking space along the California coastline as the sun melts into the horizon. You'll see why having a sunset view is so popular.

After you've completed the listing agreement and talked to the sellers about what they like about their home, you should be able to give the sellers an idea of your advertising plans. Inform them of where you'll be advertising, how often and how you'll track the results of the ads. This will help to reassure them that you'll be making every effort to sell their home.

Use this form to increase your knowledge of

19

your listings and learn about special features of the property to include in your property advertising.

EXPANDED LISTING FORM

Address_____

Owner_____

Listing Agent_____

Special Features Section

(Note any special features under each heading)

Kitchen _____

Family Room_____

Living Room_____

Dining Room_____

Bedrooms _____

Master Bedroom_____

Baths_____

View_____

Location_____

Lot_____

Architecture_____

Basement_____

Garage_____

Financing_____

Taxes_____

Closets_____

Bonus Rooms_____

Condition _____

Fencing _____

Flooring _____

Windows _____

Heating, Air Conditioning, Plumbing,
    Electrical _____

Pool, Spa, Tennis Court _____

Appliances _____

Energy Saving Features _____

Security System _____

Colors/Wallcoverings _____

What Did Owner Enjoy Most About This
    Home? _____

_____

Now you've completed the first part of your homework: You've familiarized yourself with your listing and its possible benefits. The second part of your homework is to find out what features sell in your area and therefore, what features you should emphasize (or not mention) in your ad.

    Besides your own experience, you can use local or national research sources to learn what features are currently popular with home buyers in your area. Many local newspapers conduct their own research and make this information available to their advertisers. Also the National Association of Realtors (NAR), National Asso-

Know What Features Sell

21

ciation of Home Builders (NAHB), your local Board of Realtors or even interior decorating firms may have some interesting statistics for you.

For example, in one survey by the *New York Times*, 54 percent of home buyers in the New York metropolitan area said they seek a neighborhood or location as their prime factor in determining what home to purchase.

Another survey, by the *St. Petersburg Times* and *Evening Independent*, breaks down home buyers by age categories. For example, 80 percent of their home buyers under 35 years old were attracted by a home's price and terms. For those 65 and over, only 42 percent thought that price and terms were important.

In a survey done by Great Western Real Estate in California, only two percent of the home buyers would choose a one-car garage to receive a $3,000 to $4,000 discount from a similar home with a two-car garage. Consequently, advertising that a listing has a one-car garage is probably more of a deficit than a benefit in Southern California.

The *San Diego Union* and *Tribune* try to keep their real estate classified advertisers informed through a monthly *Trends* newsletter. A recent issue of the publication stated that wall-to-wall carpeting, fluorescent lighting and earth-tones were out. Wood floors, skylights and pastels were mentioned as the newest decorating trends among home buyers. All of these surveys help the listing agent to know what to advertise about the listing and what to omit.

If you're still not sure about the market for a particular home after doing some research, or if you think the home might appeal to several markets (such as empty-nesters as well as newlyweds), you can conduct some research of your own. Try creating several ads with headlines that appeal to a particular segment of the market. For example:

Now That the Kids Are Gone...
or
The Perfect Starter Home...

In order for an ad to result in a positive response, it must address a reader's needs and wants either rationally or emotionally. Learn what these appeals are and use them often in all of your ads.

Consider the reasons (change in lifestyle, for example) that people buy homes and be sure to address these reasons, right in your headlines if you can. Following are some lifestyle changes that prompt people to buy or sell their homes:

- Growing family
- Shrinking family (empty-nesters)
- Divorce
- Marriage
- Increase in income
- Decrease in income (retiring)
- New interests (tennis, golf, recreational needs)

Turning Shoppers Into Buyers

Some ad writers spend so much time on their headlines that they fall apart when it comes time to write the rest of the ad. The most important point to remember is to support the head with the copy. These ads were submitted by the MacDonald Classified Service. Here, the first line of the body copy builds directly on the appeal made in the headline.

REACH FOR THE STARS!

You're almost there with this NEW LISTING on 2.7 acres at the top of the mountain in Meadow Creek. Only 1 year old, this exquisitely appointed custom colonial offers many of the gracious features of a bygone era: deep crown moldings, solid oak cabinetry, oversized rooms, a private screened porch — even a butler's pantry. The convenience and comfort of the 80's can be found in the designer kitchen and baths, large functional family areas, efficient gas heat and super sized garage and storage spaces. Excellent schools, shopping, and recreation nearby. $203,000. Call for an appointment.

First Lastname
(O) Office Phone   (H)Home Phone

YOURNAME

- Need for low or no maintenance (older couples or young couples who both work)
- Change in climate
- Job change (relocation or move closer to the city)
- Income tax benefits
- Need for security, health services or proximity to churches or schools

Now, look *behind* the reasons to all the emotional factors that go into a home purchase. As you know, these emotional "needs" often are the ones that turn shoppers into buyers:

- Pride of ownership (causes a renter to become a homeowner)

- Sudden affluence (and the need to demonstrate success to all those who know him)
- Investment appeal (the fact that most of the country's wealthiest families became rich by owning or developing real estate)
- Newness (and the need for change — the same way people like to buy new clothes to have the latest fashion)
- U.S. economy ("now's the time to buy" because of favorable interest rates and other indicators or "now may be the last time to buy" because interest rates are going up)
- Value (and everyone's desire to get a true bargain)

Armed with this knowledge, you can choose which benefits are most likely to appeal to your potential buyers and flag down these readers right in the headline. For example, if your listing overlooks a golf course, has three small bedrooms and is priced "right," you might create a headline that says:

Bring Your Golf Clubs!

The Lowest Priced Golf Course Home at $80,000

The body of the ad would target the golf enthusiast and appeal to this buyer's wants and

Again, the start of the body adds a benefit to the features of the home mentioned in the head. Then the copy uses the "understood" you in the next two sentences to relate directly to the buyer's needs.

A Dramatic Floor Plan
IN A PRIME LOCATION

Ideal for entertaining. Welcome guests in a tiled foyer with soaring ceilings, double skylights and a drink from the built-in wet bar. Relax in the formal living area and enjoy the golf course vistas. The master bedroom suite includes a wonderful spa and a private courtyard. Walls of oak cabinets, a center cooking island, garden window and a tiled breakfast area make the kitchen a delightful room. Oak paneled family room with a fireplace flanked by bookshelves. There's a separate guest quarters, heat pump, just a year old. $269,000. Call First Lastname, 555-6789 or Second Lastname, 555-6789. Directions: North on Coburg, left on Cal Young, left on Spyglass to 1030

needs — a home that is close to a golf course at a low price.

Creating a benefit for the "average" house (three bedroom, two bath, one-car garage, tract home), is challenging, but particularly helpful. This house doesn't offer the features of more elaborate or custom homes, such as skylights, hot tubs, atriums, acreage, etc. that would normally attract your ad reader.

If the house is close to schools, you might feature "Your Kids Can Walk to XYZ School" in the headline. This head is better than "Three Bedrooms, Two Baths" with "close to schools" buried in the ad's body.

For example, a home with the master bedroom downstairs and three bedrooms on the second level generally doesn't appeal to a family with very young children, but is just the type of floor plan that accommodates a family with teenagers. Translate that marketing knowledge into an effective headline for the ad:

Need a Separate Floor for the Kids?

rather than:

Try This Four Bedroom on Two Levels

Notice how the first headline positions the listing as a family home and the second ad just states the features.

Here's another example. If a house can be bought with no money down (or low down payment), it should appeal to investors. Flag them down in the headline:

Investors: This One's For You

The ad could continue with a sub-headline:

No Money Down

The body of the copy should stress that the probable rental of the property is expected to cover the debt service (if that information is accurate).

Transferring a home's features into benefits is essential to writing effective ads for your listings. Using "benefit statements" in your body

**Classified
Section**

27

FROM THE TOP of the vaulted ceiling in the spacious greatroom to the tall treed lot, this home offers quality and affordability. 3 large bedrooms and roomy breakfast area off kitchen will please Mom. Double garage and lots of storage space will catch Dad's eye. Formal dining room, 2 full baths, all situated in excellent Madison location and value priced at $91,900. Call First Lastname.

YourName
PROPERTIES, 555-9876

copy goes beyond giving the buyer information on the property; the benefits can actually persuade a prospect to call or buy.

The key to remember is to ask yourself: "How does this feature really benefit someone who is going to buy the home?" Following is a list of features and how they translate into home buyer benefits to give you an idea how this system works. This list is included in *Write It & Reap*, a publication of The MacDonald Classified Service in Lafayette, Indiana.

Here's a sample worksheet that shows how features can be translated into benefits.

Feature	*Benefit*
Aluminum siding	easy maintenance
Blacktop drive	low maintenance
Brick exterior	maintenance free
Built-in bookshelves	great for storage
Ceiling fans	economical
Close-in location	convenience
Cul-de-sac	low traffic area
Eat-in kitchen	convenient

Energy-efficient furnace .... low heating bills
Extra kitchen cabinets .... more storage space
Extra insulation .... economical
Fenced-in backyard .... ideal for youngsters
Full-size basement .... extra room & storage
Garage door opener .... security/ convenience
Spa .... relaxation, prestige
Large closets .... additional storage
Large patio .... for entertaining/ relaxing
Overlooks valley .... excellent view
Oversized lot .... children's play area
Pool .... summer/family fun
Remodeled kitchen .... just like new
Skylights .... bright and cheery
Subdivision .... family neighborhood
Woodsy setting .... no need to landscape

Now that you've got the idea, try the worksheet that follows for one of your own listings. Write down the best-selling features in one column. Translate them into benefit statements in the next column. Then think of the potential buyers for the listing. And finally, narrow your potential buyers to a specific market.

Benefit Statement Listing Worksheet

Best-selling features: Benefit statements:

_____   _____
_____   _____
_____   _____
_____   _____
_____   _____
_____   _____
_____   _____

This ad makes effective use of varying type sizes and the upper case / lower case style along with ample white space that contributes to easy reading. By the way, this is a sample classified for a newspaper that doesn't allow display type, artwork or borders on its classified pages.

COMFORT
and
QUIET
A Complex with
RELAXED
LIVING
featuring STUDIO APTS.

EIGHT TREES

* Airy, decorator apts. nestled on 10 lush acres
* Refreshing spacious pool
* Relaxing recreation room with lounge & wetbar
   All air-conditioned!
   Studios, 1 & 2 Bdrms.
   FROM $190
   (FURNITURE AVAILABLE)

EIGHT TREES
0000 Eight Trees Blvd.
Interstate 5 at
Carmel Road
000-0000
An ADULT LIVING Community
NO PETS

Potential buyers:_____

_____

_____

Based on benefits of listing, who are the most likely buyers for this property?

_____

_____

_____

30

Now you know how to appeal to the specific market you've targeted for the property and to include only the highlights or features of the home that satisfy an emotional want or current trend in your classifieds. But how do you know what information to leave off? If you omit the price from the ad you are sure to turn off many readers who might respond to your ad if they had known the price. Some advertising experts claim that leaving off the listing price from the ad is like wasting money on the space.

In a survey by the *St. Petersburg Times,* 80 percent of Florida home buyers under age 35 said that they bought their home based on its price and terms. If you don't include the price of the home in a real estate ad aimed at this market, you would not be providing the essential information most buyers are looking for.

On the other hand, other sources say that leaving off the price will increase the chances that the reader will call — to learn the price if the listing sounds interesting. After all, most classifieds don't sell their listings. If your ad gets the phone to ring, even if you wind up selling the caller a different listing at a lower or higher price, it certainly qualifies as an effective ad.

You'll have to decide which method is best based on what you know about your target market and current home values in your area. If you're not sure whether or not to include the listing price, you may want to try your own marketing test by running two ads for the same property, one with the price and one without.

What *Not* to Say

This ad uses a screen over the body type only. The ad itself might fall more into the institutional category than listing advertising since two logos are included and the logos are the largest part of the ad. (This ad was submitted by MacDonald Classified Service.)

Use a different name in each ad, such as, "Ask for Betty" and "Ask for Mrs. Harper" so that you can see for yourself which ad brings in the greater response.

Another point to consider is the address of the property. Again, research has shown that most buyers have a preferred location in mind when they start looking for a home to buy and the great majority will buy in that preferred location.

A prestigious address mentioned in the headline certainly satisfies the requirement that the location be included in any listing ad. But for less desirable locations, consider the possibility of featuring a highly desirable price in the headline (rather than the problem location).

However, most classified real estate ads don't include the address unless they're written to advertise an open house. Some brokers believe that mentioning the address in the ad will work against (rather than help) getting the phone to ring. "If the shopper has the address, he doesn't need me," said one San Diego real estate broker. "He'll drive by the house himself and decide he doesn't like the outside. He'll never have the opportunity to see the interior features that might just suit his needs." The fact is most buyers are looking for a reason *not* to buy. Mentioning the address in the ad may just provide them with this reason before they've given themselves the chance to find out whether or not the home is truly right for them.

The best rule to follow in this case is don't routinely list the address of the property in the ad unless you have some compelling reason for doing so, such as a prestigious location or an exceptionally attractive or well-kept property.

Staying Out of Trouble

You've seen your listing and know the features of the home and the benefits it offers prospects. But have you given the property a reasonable inspection?

Today disclosure is an important issue in real estate — and advertising. This issue is quickly spreading throughout the country, starting with California.

Your first step in complying with disclosure requirements is to conduct a reasonable inspec-

33

tion. After the inspection, all uncovered defects of a property should be noted and discussed with the seller before any advertising begins. Can a home be advertised in "excellent condition" if the buyer later finds that a new roof is needed? What if a sales associate relies on the information provided by the seller — that his house is on a one-acre lot, for example — advertises it and then finds out that the property boundaries were mistaken?

These are some of the questions that could be resolved in court. There already are federal and state laws prohibiting false, fraudulent or misleading advertising. In addition, the Code of Ethics and Standards of Practice of the National Association of Realtors (NAR) states: "The Realtor shall be careful at all times to present a true picture in his advertising and representations to the public."

However, the Code was modified in November 1986, to say:

> [that while] "...the Realtor shall avoid exaggeration, misrepresentation, or concealment of pertinent facts relating to the property...the Realtor shall not...be obligated to discover latent defects in the property or to advise on matters outside the scope of his real estate license. The Realtor shall be obligated to discover and disclose adverse

factors reasonably apparent to someone with expertise in only those areas required by their real estate licensing authority...does not impose upon the Realtor the obligation of expertise in other professional or technical disciplines."

An interpretation by an NAR attorney pointed out that a reasonable inspection by a Realtor would not need to be of the same depth as an inspection provided by a construction engineer. The buyer of the property still has responsibility to visually inspect the property himself before buying. He probably couldn't justify (in court) buying the property based solely on its ad, without looking at the listing.

On the other hand, if you discover a defect, you don't need to advertise it. You should discuss it with the seller and let him decide if he can or wants to correct it. If it is not corrected, you should let the seller know that you will provide information on the defect on a standard disclosure form to the buyer before he signs a purchase agreement. Don't take the listing if the seller won't allow you to disclose construction defects to the buyer. That would put you — as well as the seller — at risk of legal action.

Advertising that a property is in "excellent condition" generally isn't a problem if the house has no known defects and has been regularly maintained. This wording (like the expression,

Location Isn't Everything.

but this home has it and everything else. Affordable, convenient and energy efficient. Balcony overlooks beautiful trees and lushly landscaped courtyard. $49,900. First Lastname.

Buy Of The Week

Exceptionally well-kept creekside condo in the Oaks of Preston Ridge. Many amenities - Wonderful location at a great price! CALL TODAY! low $90's First Lastname.

Care Free Living

Lovely 2-story condo overlooking the 6th green of Bent Tree Country Club. Master suite has sitting area with WBFP and balcony. Living room and den share deck, see-thru WBFP and wetbar. Kitchen with all the extras. Other features include security gate, burglar alarm, atrium, tennis courts and pool. $269,000 First Lastname.

Yourname Realtors
555-6789

"Have a good day") has come to be rather meaningless, and is not taken at face value any more.
It's better, however, to be more specific in your
advertising. For example, use:

```
25-year-old ranch, with
new roof, one-year-old dish-
washer, stove and refrigera-
tor, new carpeting and paint
```

rather than

```
25-year-old ranch in ex-
cellent condition
```

Other mentions in the NAR Code of Ethics
regarding advertising state that:

1. Realtors should ensure that their
   status as brokers or Realtors (or
   Realtor-Associates) is clearly iden-
   tifiable in advertising.
2. Prices quoted in ads should be only
   those prices that have been agreed
   upon with the owners of the properties.
3. When advertising his own property,
   his ownership and status as a Realtor or licensee should be disclosed.
4. The name of the firm holding the listing on the property should be disclosed in the ad.

Another example of "flagging down" your buyers in the headline.

1ST TIME
Home Buyers!

Save Thousands $

NEWER 3BR MID $30'S
WESTRIDGE MALL

Nice NEWER West valley neighborhood. Choice corner lot. Living room, Ariz. room, 2c carport. Xlnt value! Sold for $65,000 in 3/85.

3BR 2BA MID $40'S
FIREPLACE, AC, SOLAR

NEWER West valley neighborhood. Quality block construction. Nice front elevation on cul de sac lot. Large master suite, lrg living room, eat-in kitchen, 2c carport. Xlnt value! Sold for $61,500 in 10/84.

NEWER 3BR - $50'S
DEER VALLEY H.S.

Choice GLENDALE neighborhood. 3br, 2 baths, large living rm + family rm, AC & SOLAR. 2c carport. 1304sf. Built in 1984. Great value!

GREAT FHA TERMS!

Please call for sealed offer information.

FIRST LASTNAME

■ 555-6789 ■

REALTY COMPANY

5. Realtors should have authority from their clients before advertising the client's property.

Equal Opportunity in Housing

You should be aware that discrimination in housing is illegal. But these practices continue to this day. The parties and real estate professionals involved sometimes perpetuate discrimination very innocently and unknowingly.

To avoid it, never advertise exclusively to an ethnic, racial or even religious group. You may already know not to say "fine Jewish neighborhood" or make any reference to ethnic, racial or religious community centers or organizations in your ads. But discrimination in advertising goes beyond the wording of the ad.

For example, don't advertise a listed home that is in a heavily populated Jewish neighborhood in just the local Jewish newspapers. You could be accused of discrimination, even if you think that the Jewish community would like to be aware of this listing and may provide a likely buyer for the home.

Some racial and ethnic groups around the country have been approaching real estate agents requesting their assistance in selling homes or property exclusively to their particular group.

Realtors should not participate in trying to sell property to any one group of this nature or to advertise a property to any one group. Don't

**JUST LISTED
CAMPBELL HILLS**

CUSTOM COLONIAL AND...

THE VIEW GOES ON FOREVER! Unparalleled mountain views and a tranquil setting highlight this custom built colonial home. Features include 4 BRs, 2-1/2 baths, Foyer, Formal living and dining rooms, large EIK with separate nook and loads of oak cabinets, family room with fireplace, deck, 2-car attached garage with door openers, natural wood trim throughout and so much more you'll have to see for yourself. You'll appreciate the quality construction and numerous upgraded features the owners carefully selected. Asking $176,950, with a large VA Loan takeover available. Call me today.

**YOURNAME REALTORS
555-6789**

take a listing from any seller who tells you not to sell his home to any particular racial, ethnic or religious group or who says he will only sell his home to one group.

The "Disaster"

There's nothing illegal about advertising a "disaster." This label in an ad might attract some interest among buyers who equate "disaster" with "bargain." But what do you think the seller's reaction is going to be when he opens the classified section and sees his house labeled a "disaster" by his real estate agent?

The same holds true for phrases like "owners desperate," "all it needs is TLC" or even "handyman special." Discuss the way you will market the home with the seller when you take the listing. If the house is indeed a "fixer," tell him the marketing potential of these types of properties, when they are priced right. Be sure he is in full agreement before you start advertising this way. If you think there may be a problem in the future, get his approval of your advertising and written permission before you place the ads.

The Financing

In tough real estate markets, and in periods of high interest rates, location, location, location becomes financing, financing, financing when it comes to the main selling points of a home. Even in a normal market, good financing should be promoted. If you have a listing that can be bought with no money down or with monthly payments of $499, promote and advertise these benefits — with care.

You must comply with Regulation Z, the Truth in Lending law, when real estate financing is part of your ad. Full disclosure of the price, terms and annual percentage rate — not just the monthly payment — must be included in the ad.

Here's an example:

> **$566 a Month*** Two-bedroom condo in Winchester Estates. Cathedral ceilings, all appliances, fireplace, panoramic views.*Sales price of

AMER. RIVER CANYON
OPEN

Come see this just completed 4 bedroom on a large cul-de-sac with lavish baths, atrium, spacious kitchen and open 1-5 today! Visit 140 Silva Ct. off Waterview and priced at $259,950. Firstname 555-6789

555-9876
YOUR
NAME

REAL ESTATE

$85,500. $2,350 down payment, FHA GPM 245B, $566 principal & interest 1st year, $610 P&I 2nd year, $656 P&I 3rd year, $705 P&I 4th year, $758 P&I 5th year, $815 6th through 30th years. 10 1/4% annual percentage rate.

As you can see here, all the caveats in real estate advertising deal with disclosure in one way or another — either in informing the seller how you will market his property or in letting the buyer know that payments will increase, if indeed they will, over the life of the mortgage.

Also remember fair housing and full disclosure of known defects to the buyer. If you keep your clients' needs ahead of your own, you should be able to stay out of trouble in advertising your services and your listings.

EAST SIDE RANCH

LOW MAINTENANCE, plus 3 bedrooms, eat-in kitchen, living room with fireplace, are just a few of the features you will enjoy with this delightful home. Situated on a lovely landscaped lot on a quiet dead-end street, this home can be yours for $109,900. Call Alex or Diona, 555-6789.

DON'T DREAM TOO LONG

BECAUSE this 3 bedroom contemporary Cape, situated on a country lane in Harwinton, won't last! Sunken living room with fieldstone fireplace, French doors to covered deck, freshly wallpapered formal dining room, custom kitchen with butcher block counter tops, plus so much more! $184,900. Call Georgiann, 555-6789. TODAY!

A MUST SEE! !

BE SURE NOT TO MISS this bright, spacious 7 room Raised Ranch located in a quiet, country area, but only minutes from town! Features include fireplaced family room, formal dining room, 3 bedrooms, basement work area, plus attached garage. STILL TIME TO ENJOY THE GREAT YARD FOR SUMMER FUN! $124,900.

HARWINTON LAND

VERY SCENIC 5 ACRES in area of fine homes. Towering Pines, stream, views. COULD BE PERFECT SETTING FOR YOUR DREAM HOME! $60,000. Call Barbara, 555-6789.

PRICED RIGHT !

CAN YOU salvage this two family home that must be removed from its foundation and lot to a location of your choice? OR, perhaps you might be interested in this house for its hardwood and pine flooring, beautiful wood trim, unique older-style light fixtures, etc.... If interested CALL FOR DETAILS!

Yourname Here

real estate
555-6789

Barbara	**555-6789**
Georgiann	**555-6789**
Alex	**555-6789**
Diona	**555-6789**

Remember to advertise a range of listings in different price categories to increase the number of calls you'll get. This block ad includes homes from $60,000 to $184,000 and is sure to attract a variety of buyers. The ad also uses adequate white space around the company logotype to make the signature really stand out. (These ads were supplied by Classified International.)

THE

use

OF

news

WANT

ads

	42 Caps
72 Caps	
	42 L.C.
	36 Caps
72 L.C.	
	36 L.C.
	30 Caps
60 Caps	
	30 L.C.
	24 Caps
60 L.C.	24 L.C.
	18 Caps
48 Caps	18 L.C.
	14 Caps
	14 L.C.
	10 Caps
48 L.C.	10 L.C.
	Agate
	Agate

WILL

bring

BEST

results

FOR

you if each

ONE OF YOUR

classified ads

IS PLACED FOR

three (3) or more

CONSECUTIVE TIMES

in a classification

THAT'S APPROPRIATE FOR

all goods & services you

WISH TO OFFER! CLASSIFIED

ads are "people sized ads"

This chart shows various type sizes normally available for classified advertising.

3.
Preparing and Writing Classifieds

Every business has its own jargon. In real estate, there are mortgage terms such as ARMs (adjustable rate mortgages) and FHA-GPMs (a graduated payment mortgage insured by the Federal Housing Administration) as well as other phrases particular to the real estate business, like "handyman special" (a property requiring more work than just a fresh paint job) or "exclusive right to sell" (an agreement that allows the broker to be the sole agent of the seller and collect a fee when the property is sold regardless of who arranges the sale).

A newspaper's classified department also has its own language that should be quickly learned by any real estate professional who chooses to

Classified Language

advertise in these sections. A handy glossary of newspaper advertising terms and jargon is included at the back of this book. At first, terms like *agate, justified* and *font* may seem overwhelming, but remember that you learned all the real estate jargon and survived, so you will be capable of writing and placing your own classifieds too.

To make your job easier, several possible alternatives are available to help rookie advertisers. First, some newspapers publish their own instructional booklets or subscribe to services that can help their advertisers compose their ads. For example, the MacDonald Classified Service in Lafayette, Indiana is used by 740 newspapers. It's also available to real estate salespeople and brokers by subscription.

This service distributes information on real estate trends and reprints actual real estate classified ads that have run in newspapers across the country in a monthly newsletter format. Classified International Advertising Service in Hollywood, Florida offers a similar newsletter. The newspapers subscribe to these services and then provide the sample ads and other information to their advertisers — real estate salespeople like you.

Second, some newspapers also sponsor seminars on how to use the classified pages and how to write ads. These seminars are helpful, especially to a new advertiser or anyone who prefers to listen to instructions and ideas rather than read about them.

Third, many newspapers publish their own materials on writing effective classified ads or will write the ads for you. As tempting as it may sound, *don't* let the classified newspaper salesperson write your ads. Your brokerage and your listings are unique. You don't want them to sound like everyone else's. On the other hand, some newspapers will develop creative artwork for their advertisers at an additional charge. Take advantage of these services *if* they can provide high quality work. The newspaper's graphic arts services are generally less costly than hiring your own.

Classified Ad Rules

Most, but not all, classified sections have rules and policies you must follow. Classifieds are generally distinguished from display by their standard sized columns, restricted type style and size, and lack of any visuals (graphics, artwork or photos).

While a headline is the single most important copy element in any ad (classified or display), some classified sections don't even allow large or bold type. In those cases, the classified advertiser really has to work wonders with words to make his ads stand out.

But some classified sections do deviate, allowing borders, logos or clip art (stock pieces such as a line art drawing of a house). Find out what your paper's policies are first before writing and designing your ads.

Following are some general rules and

guidelines that will help you in working with any classified ad department.

1. Don't ask for a special space. As with most advertising, the classified department generally will not guarantee a position on the page.

On the other hand, especially in major metropolitan daily newspapers, predetermined classified listings are available. These are generally organized by the name of the suburb under which you want to advertise. For example, you could select Barrington, (near Chicago) for your ad in the *Chicago Tribune* and your ad would appear under that headline, saving you the space and cost of listing "Barrington" in your ad copy.

You may even want to advertise under more than one designated category. If your paper has separate headings for suburbs and price categories, put your listing under the right town and the right price range so readers can find your ad easily.

2. Proofread your own ads before they run and read them immediately after they're published. Newspapers will credit your account for one incorrect ad, but you'll be paying if more than one incorrect "insertion" has run. If you request a proof copy from the newspaper before your ad is published, you will have to prepare your material for an earlier deadline, so plan ahead.

3. Ask for rateholder rates. Charges for classifieds are based on the number of words, the number of lines or the number of inches. A rateholder advertiser generally is one who advertises in consecutive editions or guarantees a certain volume of advertising during the year.

In exchange for the higher volume, a discount is offered. Some newspapers offer volume rates for classified advertisers but others only offer the discounts to display advertisers. For example, the rateholder rate for a weekday three-line classified in the *Los Angeles Times* (for 30 or more consecutive days) is $6.30. That compares to the one-day rate of $10.90 for the same size ad. Newspapers also may offer "pick-up rates," a discount for picking up the ad and repeating it without any changes. While setting type for the ad is included in the space rate, repeating the same copy saves the newspaper the costs of changing the type, so ask if a pick-up rate is available.

If your ad has pulled in a good response, there may be no need to change it. You could repeat the ad until the listing is sold or until the ad no longer pulls a response.

4. Know the deadlines. Deadlines don't just apply to reporters. While newspapers tend to extend their deadlines as long as possible to accommodate their advertisers (some newspapers accept ads over the telephone), final deadlines are strictly followed.

To help you meet deadlines, some newspapers offer free pick up and delivery service for copy, proofs or tearsheets (a page torn out of the publication to show the advertiser that the ad has actually appeared).

5. Inquire about block ads. These are used to run a number of listings under your logo or name. They save money because you only pay for the space for your logo once, rather than with each ad.

Block ads are effective in your local newspaper. But if you're advertising several properties, each in a different community in a metropolitan daily, keep each listing under its location heading instead of grouping them under your logo. The reader will never find your ads under the community he's interested in and he'll be confused.

In some cases, however, the competition may cause you to run your logo as often as you can on the classified advertising pages, simply because everyone else is.

Copy-writing

Numerous formulas and acronyms for writing ad copy have been suggested and followed over the years, but for writing and designing classifieds, all that you really need to know is:

- Get Their Attention
- Give Them the Benefits
- Close for Action

You'll lose your classified reader before he has a chance to call if you don't get his attention through an outstanding headline (or the first few words of the body copy if the newspaper doesn't allow headlines). Think of the headline as the grabber. But if you can't use your own headline, you can still get a response.

Consider that a newspaper reporter never writes his own headline for his story. Headline writing is assigned to the copyeditor. So the reporter attracts attention to his story by writing the best "lead" (first sentence) that he can. Reporters notoriously pour over their leads, refining them until they are razor sharp, with not one excess word.

In recent times, even phrases (not grammatically complete sentences) have become acceptable leads that sometimes begin award-winning pieces of journalism. The reason for this casual writing style is that reporters want to communicate with their readers as effectively as possible. They'll use whatever approach achieves bright, refreshing and attention-getting copy.

Another old tradition in the journalism business is the "inverted pyramid." That means that everything following the lead in the story falls into a pattern of an inverted pyramid — the most important information closest to the top of the story, with layers of supporting details following in descending order of importance. The least relevant information should be at the end of the story.

That style is generally used for two reasons. First, the writer never knows if his story is going to be cut for space requirements so the least important information should be at the end, in case the length needs to be cut.

Second, the writer also knows that his article is competing with every other article and ad on the page for the reader's attention. Chances are he may lose the reader to another article or ad before the whole story is read. Consequently, he had better give the reader some sound information before the reader jumps to the next story.

In writing a classified ad, limited space and competition are even more of a concern. Learning the technique of writing leads and writing in an inverted pyramid will certainly help you to gain attention and make sure you've given the most important information about the listing in the ad. That's why you shouldn't cloud your thoughts with every detail about the listing. Concentrate on the major benefits a home buyer will achieve.

After you've written your ad copy, do what the reporters do and start cutting out excess words. You can use this system until you become more familiar with thinking and writing with as few words as possible.

Now that you know you must attract the reader's attention immediately, how do you accomplish it? First, always use a headline if the classified section allows it. Make your headlines a labor of love, just like the big-time ad agencies do. The head alone has the biggest impact on "pulling power" for the whole ad. An ad that doesn't pull won't make the phone ring or the listing sell. And if one headline doesn't say as much as you'd like, try two — a head and a subhead.

Unfortunately, as important a tool as the head is, it is still the most misunderstood and abused part of real estate classified advertising. Following are some headlines, picked at random from classified sections. Think about the market they have targeted or the benefits they have offered the reader about the listing. My comments are in parentheses.

Your Attention-Getting Headline

L-O-V-E

(Who's in love: the broker with the listing? The owner with his house?)

I Want You

(For what? Why should the reader care?)

Seller Says Sell

(Doesn't he have anything better to say?)

Interest Rates Climbing

(Believe it or not, some broker used this head while the rest of the industry was trying to convince buyers that interest rates were affordable. When the reader sees this head, he'll think he can't afford a home.)

Make an Offer

(Why? What does this home offer?)

A Joy to See

(Really says nothing)

If these listing agents had thought about the market for the home and positioned the home for that market, they never would have used these headlines.

Equally meaningless are headlines like "Fantastic, Beautiful, Gorgeous." These overused adjectives say nothing about the homes or the buyer you hope to seek.

Now that you have some ideas on what not to do, consider these headlines (Again, my comments are in parentheses.):

Room Outside for RV
Space Inside for Big Family

(This head includes a benefit to RV owners

or others who need outside storage out of view. The second line targets the market for the home. Anyone who has one of these needs will certainly read this ad.)

Ideal for Entertaining

(Appeals to those families or executives who have this need.)

No Qualifying

(Flags down buyers who can't get new financing.)

Remodeler's Delight
Priced Right

(This catchy two-line rhyme reaches two markets: those who enjoy decorating and buyers who want a bargain.)

Contemporary Ranch

(Most buyers want a new house. "Contemporary" indicates that the home is new or decorated in a more modern style and appeals to this emotional need. Surveys also show that nationally, most home buyers want a single-level home. Putting this benefit — ranch — in the head attracts this substantial market.)

Less Than Rent

(Obviously offers financial incentive to the renter.)

Build the Benefits in Body Copy

Now that you've written a headline that really grabs your reader's attention, don't lose your momentum in your supporting body copy. This is tricky in the classified section because you're trying to make benefits out of features in a condensed space. Remember your inverted pyramid style: Make sure that the main features are mentioned first followed by a few amenities in descending order of importance.

One of the biggest mistakes some listing agents make is starting their ad with an attention-getting bang, but then continuing with body copy that doesn't support the head. Take a look at these examples:

```
Ocean View
2BR 2 ba, Oak Floors,
New Kitchen
```

(The two-line copy doesn't add any information about the benefits of the view.)

```
Your Best Investment
Great Location, 2 BR
Air-conditioned
```

(How do the location and other features add up to a great investment?)

> **Enjoy Golf?**
> Like-new 3 BR 2 ba
> Wood siding

(Where's the golf course?)

Your ad copy should sustain, not divert, the attention your headline succeeded in getting. Then be sure to include the facts every home buyer wants to know — number of bedrooms, baths and the price. Consider this ad (and comments):

> **Country Charmer**
> Away from the hustle and bustle with one acre for your garden, kids and animals! 2 bedroom, 2 bath has massive brick fireplace, decorated in warm woods throughout. Below market value at $84,900.

(Note how the country theme was carried throughout the ad.)

Here are some guidelines to keep in mind when writing your classified ads.

1. Use a conversational writing style for a refreshing change from the typical want ad jargon. Also, feel free to use adjectives. They add to the emotions that you're trying to build in your ad. Take your reader on a tour, rather than just listing rooms or amenities.

2. Don't ruin your body copy with excessive abbreviations. Again, research has proven that too many abbreviations will turn off and confuse buyers. Rather than saving money for the advertiser, these ads will cause the reader to move on to another ad.

If you must abbreviate, the MacDonald Classified Service notes that ten abbreviations have been used so often in classifieds that readers generally are no longer confused by them. These words are:

approx. (approximately)
Ave. (avenue)
Blvd. (boulevard)
bldg. (building)
condo (condominium)
rec. room (recreation room)
refrig. (refrigerator)
Rd. (road)
sq. ft. (square foot)
St. (street)

3. Be sure your copy is not only completely

accurate, but also believable. Unfortunately, real estate clients are often skeptical that you won't sell their house at their price or that they'll wind up paying more for a house if they use your services.

Providing complete and specific descriptions that can be proven, will help combat this skepticism and increase the results from your ads. The words "enormous property" should be replaced by "four-acre lot." "Terrific bargain" is meaningless. "$10,000 under market value" is exact.

Even if all your claims are true, read your ad again to see whether they'll be believable. Your response will be limited if no one believes your ads.

4. Use short sentences. In advertising copywriting, anything goes, as long as it communicates. Even a one-word sentence is acceptable if that one-word line gives just the impact that is needed. Consider: "Owner is being transferred and needs to move right away." (This is quoted from an actual newspaper classified ad.)

Compare that statement to: "Price reduced to sell fast." This second sentence is shorter, has more punch and offers the benefit of a better price. Remember, buyers are interested in benefits that satisfy their own wants and needs — not the seller's situation.

5. When you have many listings to advertise, don't duplicate your efforts. Advertise one listing in each price range. Remember that the ad may not sell the listing, but should at least make the phone ring.

   A buyer who's looking for a home at a certain price will only call you once. If you advertise three homes priced at $100,000, you'll only get calls from buyers in that price range.

   If you place three ads, one each for listings at $100,000, $150,000 and $200,000, you'll get calls from three different groups of buyers. That increases your response from the same number of ads.

6. Terms like "New on the Market" or "Just Listed" do appeal to buyers who want to be the first to see a listing. Many shoppers are simply attracted to new products. Think about how many products advertise that they are "Now Improved" and how many ads start with "Introducing." Their ad agencies or research departments have proven that new or changed products are more easily remembered and are more attractive to the consumer.

   In the real estate market, think about how many area homeowners flock to see a new housing development even when they weren't in the market for a home.

"New" is definitely a plus. If you're lucky enough to have a new listing or newer home to sell, announce this information in the headline or first few words of the body copy of your ad.

7. Talk to your readers one-on-one. Most ads are read in the privacy of the reader's home—not in a stadium. Addressing the readers in the second person as "you," rather than in the third person as "home buyers" or another anonymous group, helps them immediately identify with the benefits you are trying to sell in the ad.

Consider: "Bring your family" compared to "Families are invited." The first phrase is more direct and talks directly to the reader.

8. Feel free to mention brand names. Capitalize on all the advertising that major name brand companies do to promote their products. Jenn-air cooktops mean distinction in the kitchen. Hot Spring Spa is a well-known west coast spa manufacturer that promotes economy in operation. Armstrong floors are durable and beautiful. Names of certain builders or architects in your area may stand for quality. If so, use those names in the ads for your listings.

Now Close for Action

Always end your ad with the property's listing price, your company name and phone number (unless you have set your ads in a block under your company logo or have mentioned the price earlier in the ad).

Don't end your ad with the anonymous: "Broker 299-3200." Readers aren't sure if the home belongs to a broker and by not mentioning the name of the firm, you are losing an opportunity to increase your own name recognition in the community.

While price, name and phone number are essential, you also want to give your best effort to motivate the ad reader to action — in this case, calling your office. If you've set a mood in your ad, sum up the mood again in the close. Consider:

Capture the country feeling for $___

Exquisite luxury at $___

If the strongest benefit of the listing is affordability, restate the value in the close. Some examples:

An exceptional value at $___

A hard-to-believe find at only $___

A large home at the small price of $___

In your closing, try for an immediate response. Strong ways of closing the ad with the price include:

This one won't last at $___

Call now for an immediate showing $___

Don't wait, it'll be too late $___

If you haven't grouped your listings in a block under your name or logo, be sure your name (or logo) is prominently featured at the end of your classified. That's your signature and the reader should find it easily in your ad. Also include your phone number.

Using white space around your company name (one line above and below) helps make your signature stand out. Bold face, larger type size, all upper case lettering, using your logo or centering your name are other ways to make it more striking.

Don't Forget Your Name

After you've written your head, body and close, check your ad. Does it grab your attention? Offer any benefits? Lead you to make an immediate response?

Congratulations! But, don't get so excited that you leave the office for the nearest newspaper. The next important step is to tighten your copy any way you can. Make every word count. You are trying to tell a story with your ad, but

Edit, Proof and Design

remember that classified readers are used to reading phrases or even one word sentences, rather than paragraphs.

Consider the two classified ads for the same listing which appear on the following page. The first ad ran in a newspaper. Notice how tightening it and reorganizing it with the inverted pyramid (main benefits or features listed first in the body) creates the much more readable, finished ad in the second example.

Unfortunately, the first writer starts his interior description of the home with the entrance hall. How many buyers choose a home based on its entrance hall?

Green Valley

New price on this Victorian splendor constructed of old brick and situated on approximately 4 acres affording much privacy in a convenient Green Valley location. This lovely home contains entrance hall with beautiful stairway, very large living room with fireplace, separate formal dining room, paneled den, separate breakfast room overlooking rolling lawn and woods, large paneled playroom with fireplace and bookcases, separate laundry room, two-car garage with workshop, back stairway and screened porch. Other attractive features in this 4 bedroom, 3-1/2 bath home are hardwood floors throughout, new oil furnace and recent outside painting. $l89,500. XYZ Realty 324-6000.

Here's the edited and condensed version:

Privacy Priced Right

Reduced price on this brick Victorian with approx. 4 woodsy acres in Green Valley. Wood floors complement paneled den and playroom with fireplace and built-in bookcases. For formal entertaining, try 15 x 20 ft. living room with fireplace and separate dining room. Enjoy casual meals in sunny breakfast room or private screened porch. Give your family all the room they need with 4 bedrooms, 3-1/2 baths and 2 car garage with workshop or storage area. See this two-story charmer today: $189,500. XYZ Realty 324-6000

The second ad leaves off the stairway, entrance hall and laundry room — all features of the home, but not really significant benefits to the buyer. The first ad was really just a listing of every feature the home had. The writer didn't take the time to decide which of those features a buyer is going to be interested in and didn't tie them together with a central theme.

Notice how the closing word "charmer" in the second ad relates back to the Victorian mood created in the first line of the body copy in the ad. Also instead of the "very large" living room mentioned in the first ad, exact measurements are used in the second ad. Always try to use the exact or close approximate dimensions of the lot, the home or the rooms, when you can. Very large to one person is small to someone else. Using the measurements prevents this misunderstanding.

In describing a home, consider what 2,000

square feet means to someone in a 1,400 square foot condo compared to someone in a 3,000 square foot house. Would they both think your listing was a "large" house?

Also look at the sentence structure in the first ad compared to the second. Notice how long the second sentence is in the first ad. By the time you get to the end of the sentence, can you remember how it started? Without exception, always use short sentences or phrases. (In spite of what your English teacher said, you don't have to use complete sentences in writing advertising copy).

Now focus on the appearance of your ad. How does the first ad compare to the second? The first looks long and gray — too long for the classified reader who has a dozen more ads to review before deciding which ones to call.

What makes the second ad look more inviting? White space. It's sometimes difficult for novice advertisers to accept the fact that buying nothing (no artwork or type) is their best buy for selling more homes. White space on the classified pages is the single biggest graphic device you can use to attract attention to your ads.

Some classified sections allow advertisers to use logos, borders or even halftones (reproduced photographs). Others claim that their clean and simple requirements help keep your costs down, and allow no graphic devices except white space. Remember that white space, like any graphic element, should be used to increase readability, clarity and sales. Creativity for the sake of just being original is wasted if it doesn't achieve these results. Following are some ideas on effective ways to use white space in your classifieds:

1. Use one line of space above or below your headline or subhead for added emphasis.

2. Center your company name with a line of space above and below to attract attention.

3. Divide long copy into paragraphs and use a line of space between them.

4. Try indenting your copy from the right and left margins for a distinctive look.

You can also increase readability by carefully selecting type size (some newspapers don't allow type style choices) and using upper and lower case, rather than all capitals, especially with long words or copy. Any increase in type size and lines of white space will cost a little more, but if they increase the ad's effectiveness and response, use them!

Still Don't Know Where to Start?

In the appendices, you will find a variety of headlines, some benefits and descriptions for body copy and closing statements that you can plug into your own classifieds. The number of bedrooms and baths or locations may change with each listing, but the basic appeals (to a family, investor, first-time buyer, etc.) of many of your listings are the same. Use these headlines, descriptions and closings until you feel comfortable creating your own ads.

4.
Your Competition Uses It — Display Advertising for Listings

Any advertising that doesn't follow the policies of a newspaper's classified section and generally isn't located in the classified section is called display advertising. As the name "display" implies, these ads also typically use illustrations or other graphic devices to attract attention. In many newspaper classified sections, even logos aren't allowed.

Some of the visual tools that can be used in display ads include:

- white space
- variety of type styles and sizes
- halftones (photographs) in either black-and-white or color
- line drawings
- reverse type (white type on black background)

- colored ink
- two-column or larger size ads
- borders

But before you cancel all of your classifieds for the next year, take the time to learn how these tools can be used effectively. Don't immediately conclude that only display ads will allow you to use your powerful imagination and make you appear more professional, competent and successful. You may not want to use display advertising at all for your listings.

Two of the main reasons for using display ads are market and economic conditions. That means if most of your competition is using display ads, you may be forced to follow the crowd in a tough market and use display ads for listings, open houses and your image. If you can afford the more expensive costs for display ads, use them regularly along with your classifieds for listings.

Using Newspaper Display Ads

For most real estate professionals, however, the best use of display ads is for institutional advertising or image building impact rather than for individual listings. The reason is that home buyers are accustomed to looking at the classified sections, not necessarily the rest of the newspaper, for homes for sale. Unless your display ad appears in the Homes section, they probably won't see it.

Furthermore, a big ad doesn't always increase the response. Many brokers or salespeople who have tried advertising the average listing in a display ad say that they received about the same number of inquiries from the display position as the classified section.

In his book, *Ogilvy on Advertising*, David Ogilvy also points out that two-page spreads seldom get twice the readership of full-page ads, although they cost double. So unless you have sound reasons for using long copy, think twice before doing so.

Some brokers buy display space (outside the classified section) and then compose the ad as if it was a block of listings in the classified section. This helps set their listings apart from the large volume in the classified section. But don't forget that most serious home buyers go directly to the classifieds. If you don't advertise there, you'll completely miss this market.

A clever way to use display ads for listings and at the same time attract classified readers is to request that your ad be placed opposite the start of the classifieds. However, this only works if your newspaper doesn't have a completely separate classified section, which most metropolitan dailies do.

Besides display ads that really look and act like classifieds, there are classified ads placed on the classified pages that look like display ads. These are actually called *display classified*. They have the appearance of display ads that would be placed anywhere in the newspaper, but they offer the cost advantages and identical

Following are some sample display ad sizes available in the Los Angeles Times. These sizes show the impact on the page that various sizes achieve.

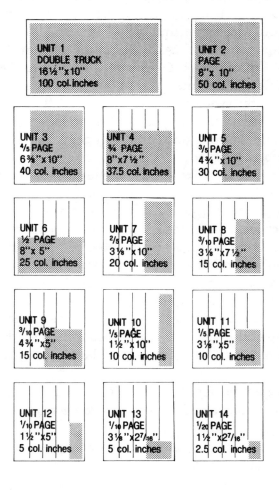

readership of classifieds. Using display classifieds will make your ads stand out in the gray sea of other brokers' listings on the classified pages. But not all newspapers offer display classifieds.

Should you use display space to advertise one listing in the local newspaper? Generally, no. However, be prepared for some sellers to ask for this treatment in marketing their home. So plan your rationale in advance to combat this request.

Once a seller feels confident that you will have more effective strategies for obtaining qualified buyers, such as marketing to other agents and classified advertising, he'll stop insisting that his home receive special, expensive display ads.

But there definitely are certain properties that are appropriate for display ads. For example, a home's unique features or high asking price may mean that the property appeals to a limited market and will endure a long listing period.

If the home could benefit from strong visual promotion or even interior photographs in the ads, you may be able to impress the sellers by using a display ad and at the same time, attract the right buyer for the property.

If you have an unusual listing — a home priced well above the median for your area or one that appeals to a special market such as senior citi-

Special Homes

zens, golfers or horse lovers — you could place a display ad in a special interest publication.

Newspapers are read by the masses — rich and poor, educated and nearly illiterate. That's why newspapers are the best way to reach the entire community. But if you have a property that has marketing appeal to only a small segment of the community, the magazine is often a better choice for your display ad.

Look for local special interest magazines and write an ad that appeals to their readers. The following example is a listing ad for a senior citizen magazine:

Meet New Friends

Get ready for an active social life at this all-adult community with pool, rec. center and planned events. Your new ranch-style home features low maintenance yard, bright kitchen with modern appliances, air conditioning for cool summers and two bedrooms, two easy-care baths. Health services are within a few blocks for expert medical care.

Call today, see tonight!

(Photograph)

Linda Lipman Real Estate
321-4000

Notice that this ad was written exclusively to attract the senior market. As each feature of the home was chosen, it was amplified to include a specific benefit of that feature. The ad also asks for action in the close before the signature of the company. This ad is more appropriate for the senior magazine than the general circulation newspaper.

Advertising Open Houses

While classified ads are frequently written to announce open houses, many real estate agents are starting to use display ads for this purpose. Open houses fall more into the pattern of traditional retail display advertising in that you are offering a product "on sale" for a short time only — this Sunday or Saturday. Readers respond well to department store ads that announce one-day-only sales.

Advertising an open house in a display space exclusively, offers you the opportunity to chart an accurate response to your display ad since you can judge for yourself how many buyers come to the open house. You can then try another open house in the classified section and measure your response. Since newspapers and competition vary around the country, this test of classified versus display advertising for the open house is the best way to see if the display ad is useful to you.

Be sure your open house ad says just that — Open for Inspection, Open House, Open This Sunday or some similar identifying phrase. It should also include the hours, the address or location, price and prominent features or bene-

When price. . . or even monthly payment . . . is the most attractive benefit of a property, feature it prominently as this ad does. When including financing however, you must comply with all disclosures including sales price, down payment and other terms.

Two & Three Bedroom Condominium Homes in Rancho San Diego!

$567/mo*

OVER 250 HOMES SOLD, COME SEE WHY!

From $85,500

YourName Realty

Models open 11am-6pm,
Closed Thursday
VA NO DOWN,
FHA AVAILABLE

■ YourName Realty is so successful because each distinctive floorplan includes a fireplace, built-in washer, dryer and microwave.

■ Other features include: a large private park, panoramic views, huge pool & tennis courts

Sales price $85,500, $2,350 Down Payment, FHA GPM 245B, $567 Principal & Interest 1st year, $610 P&I 2nd year, $656 P&I 3rd year, $705 P&I 4th year, $758 P&I 5th year, $815 6th-30th years. Closing costs, taxes, mutual mortgage insurance and homeowners dues additional. 10 1/4% Annual Percentage Rate.

fits to bring in buyers. Besides the brokerage, you could also list the name of the sales associate holding the open house in the ad. It's better to use a picture of the featured property, rather than a picture of the listing agent.

Although you are using the display space to advertise a listing — and hopefully to get a sale — you also are increasing the awareness of your image in the community. If you advertise a listing and your phone doesn't begin to ring immediately, you may still gain some advantage. People who see your listing ads will start to get an impression of your firm and your ability as a listing agent.

Is it for Your Image or for the Sale?

If your ads are well done and consistent over time, people will start believing that you are successful. They will see a representation of the types of homes you have listed and they'll think you could sell their home just as easily.

Display ads for listings may be the only display ads you ever place, and therefore, the only institutional ads your market sees. Many brokers — and especially salespeople — don't place traditional institutional ads. If that's the case with you, make your display ads for listings and open houses shine!

You've got your copy (the written message for your ad), but how's your ad going to look and where's it going to go (what publication)?

Designing Ads

Advertisers spend millions of dollars trying to get the right readers to notice their ads. Part of that money goes into designing the ads. In ad agency art departments, creative people try to make their ad copy visually attractive so readers will actually read the entire ad. That's a big challenge. How many ads have you read recently beyond the headline?

Decisions on borders, type style, size, photographs or drawings all must be made. But these are generally not the type of decisions that are best made by the ad copywriter. If you've written your own display ad, you've accomplished a lot. Thinking that you can lay out the ad in a professional manner is a little over ambitious if you're inexperienced.

The most common mistake is to crowd the ad with too much copy, thinking that you want to get the most for your money. Often, the result is that none of the ad gets read because it looks long and boring to the reader.

One way to avoid these mistakes is to work with an experienced freelance or newspaper production artist. You can still make the final decision on what the ad will look like but you'll also have the benefit of a professional's advice.

However, if you use the production department at the newspaper, you may find that your ad looks like everyone else's. By using an outside artist, you will have more type and graphic arts choices. However, don't get carried away with being too creative. Unusual layouts may get noticed, but they don't always sell products.

Following are some tried-and-true pointers to help you design your own ad or to make the right decisions when working with a professional. Whether you choose to work alone or with a professional, these pointers will help to increase the visual impact of your display ads and get your message read and remembered:

Use Readable Headlines
Make your headline as long as you need to get your message across. But use upper and lower case (instead of all capitals) in all long headlines. A long head in all caps is more difficult to read quickly. You can also try putting your headline in quotes to increase the recall power of your ad.

Use Photographs or Drawings
Photographs are generally better remembered than drawings. But before you decide to use photos, check how the photographs look in the publication you'll be using. Most black-and-white photographs will reproduce better if they have a high contrast (blacker blacks and whiter whites), rather than an overall gray appearance. The newspaper reproduction process tends to muddy black-and-white photos.

If that will be the case with your photo, substitute a high-quality line shot (camera-ready black ink drawing). If you don't have the budget for original artwork, newspapers or graphic arts studios can show you a book of "clip art." You pay a minimal amount for the art and simply clip it from the book and paste it into your

These are examples of camera - ready clip art to use with display ads or as headings in the classified section. These examples were supplied by The MacDonald Classified Service.

ad. You may find a line drawing of a house in the book that you can use in your ad.

Put People in the Picture

Pictures are important — but expensive. Combined with the headline, they are the two main elements that will draw readers into your copy. Studies show that people look at the illustration, then read the headline.

In your photos, use subjects that people can relate to. If you're using interior shots of a house, put a person in the photo — or better yet, a baby or an animal. People never seem to tire of looking at cute babies and cuddly pets. It's also a good idea to use a woman as a subject in the photo. Since women are the main decision makers when it comes to buying the family home, the women readers will identify with the woman in the picture.

When you're using pictures of the exteriors of homes, be sure the reader can see the house. Too many pictures of listings have overgrown shrubbery covering the house or three-quarters of the photo shows only sky because the photo was shot at a bad angle.

Use Color for Effect

Using four color (a technical term, representing yellow, magenta, cyan and black that combine for full color effect) costs at least 50 percent more than black-and-white. But twice as many people will remember a full-color photo over a black-and-white one.

However, the problem with reproducing four color is that separations of each color must be made and overlapped on top of each other to produce the final full-color photograph. Sometimes the separations shift out of registration and the picture appears out of focus. Find out in advance what compensation the paper will offer you if your color photograph reproduces badly.

Another way of using color is to use two color (rather than four color). If a newspaper is using another color (like red, blue or green) for another ad or for the banner (nameplate) that day, you may be offered that same color to highlight your headline, print your logo or other portions of your ad — at no additional charge. That's usually an excellent buy. But don't go overboard on your use of the second color. Keep your body copy in black, because most people are accustomed to reading newspapers, magazines or books that are printed in black ink.

Use a Layout That Leads the Reader
A layout that's easy to read and follow includes the photo on top, the headline under it and the body copy directly below the head. All of these elements of the ad layout (along with white space) should work together to convey the message of the ad.

This easy layout keeps the eye moving naturally from top to bottom. The headline often can serve as the caption to the photo as well. If your ad features more than one photo, use captions under each picture.

Captions have high readership, so make the most of them and include good, brief descriptions with the price (if you're showing a house). You can use this type of layout over and over again, substituting different photos and properties and grouping them by price, style or community.

Pick a Distinctive But Readable Typeface

Most newspapers use serif type rather than non-serif type. Serif type has little line endings on each letter, for example, **A**. Non-serif type doesn't have these line endings, for example, **A**.

Using the type style that readers are accustomed to seeing helps increase readability. A fancy type house may offer 1300 or more styles, but only a few are in regular use. While special typefaces are distinctive and can be used effectively for headlines, standard serif type has a higher readability for long body copy.

Work with the type house to select a headline type style that complements the style you are using for the body copy. Once you select a type style, use it consistently in all of your ads. A type style can have the same effect as a logo. If people keep seeing the same style, they will identify it with your company often without having to read your company name in the ad.

This display ad divides its space equally between an institutional message first and listings for sale on the lower half. For many real estate professionals, combining both messages works well.

Bigger is not always better!
100's
of Homeowners know!
They bought or sold their homes through
— *YourName Realty*
Join the <u>growing satisfied list — Call today!</u>

Photo Here

FELICITA VILLA Large 2 story condo, 3 BR, 2 1/2 BA, private patio, well decorated. Fireplace, balcony. POOL, SPA. $89,900.

2 ON 1 3 BR house plus 1 BR, BA, living room & kitchen in guest house. On 1/3 acre w/avos. Vista. $139,900.

YourName Realty

R When only
REALTOR Positively the best will fill the need.

HILLTOP — 2 STORY Cape Cod style — very bright & cheerful, only 3 yrs. old. 3 bedrooms (1 down) and 2 baths, French doors, deck front & back. $149,500.

2750 SQ. FT. ON 1 ACRE 2 story with 3 large bedrooms, 2 1/2 baths. Formal dining, family room, sewing room, nook. Generous use of imported tile. $197,900.

1 ACRE LOT SW Escondido - High School area. Filled with mature avocados. Natural gas! $87,900

555-7899

Consider Ads That Look Like Text

This tip pertains mostly to full-page ads that you may want to use on occasion. Making your ad look like part of the editorial section of the publication has some merit because people are more likely to read the articles in a publication and skip the ads. If you use this type of layout, follow the general style of the publication in which you're advertising. If the publication generally uses three columns of type, use three columns for your copy.

For long copy, many publications use subheads spaced throughout a long article to break up the gray space of the copy. You can use the same technique with your ad copy. If you have a few key points to make, set them off with bullets. Remember, few readers will read through an entire copy-filled ad. But with key points set off in bold face and bulleted, the reader can get your important information quickly and easily.

Pick a Good Position

Very few companies or individuals can afford to run full-page ads all the time, and the double-truck (two-page spread) is an even rarer luxury, especially for real estate firms.

In magazines, the preferred (and higher priced) positions for full-page ads are the inside cover, inside back cover and outside back cover. They are normally in color, which increases the costs to advertisers even more. The first page (if it's an ad) also commands a higher price. Natu-

Since all the copy of this display ad is in reverse, the message does get a little difficult to read. Don't you think? (This ad was supplied by Classified International)

"Via Mesa Estates"
Take your choice!
$80,900

Over 135 homes sold our first year!
Builder pays $1,500 toward closing costs.

THE ST. MICHAELS

Constant Branch, Maryland's most successful new community, has four unique home designs. Each with standard features like finished family rooms, large eat-in kitchens with modern Whirlpool appliances, a Carrier heat pump, wall-to-wall carpeting and 2 or 2½ baths.

THE JAMES

Enjoy the Constant Branch setting, in a richly wooded stream valley, perfect for a swimming or tennis afternoon. And stay close to the places you need to be. Constant Branch is convenient to major shopping centers, local merchants and excellent schools, one minute to I-95, 15 minutes from the Beltway and just 35 minutes from the Inner Harbor. Constant Branch is a place you'll be proud to call home!

THE KENT

THE POTOMAC

YourName Reality

(garages optional)

rally, larger ads receive more attention because of their sheer size, but through creative use of space, smaller ads can attract their share of attention as well.

Readership is always higher on odd-numbered, right-hand pages, so request these if you can. You can be almost assured of being dominant on a page if you choose a bottom two-thirds space, the lower half, a half page vertical or even the outside third of adjoining pages.

Your ad will surely stand out if it's the only one on the page (adjoining editorial space). If you have a smaller space (like one-sixth page), placing it on the upper right of a right-hand page is a good way to make sure it gets noticed.

Request that your ad run next to editorial space, rather than surrounded by other ads. It's even better if the ad can be at the top of a column next to editorial matter. Papers may charge extra for preferred positions because the ads are more likely to be seen. But if you can attract more readers and get more calls, preferred positions usually are worth the extra cost.

If you can't decide which is the best way to go, spend some time with the publication and see for yourself which positions you notice first. Make notes and check the "rate card" to see if the paper charges more for these positions.

Make Your Ad Stand Out

You should also consider using design tools like white space, screens and borders when they are

PACIFIC BEACH

UNLIMITED COMFORT

in a

LIMITED EDITION

*Good use of
white space,
bullets and
change in type
sizes.*

Our Adult Living Community still features BRAND NEW 1 & 2 bdrm. units designed for the descriminating resident.

*Color coordinated interiors with plush pile carpeting, wallpaper accents; many with slope beamed ceilings.

*Quality security locks & smoke detectors thru-out.

*Ample storage & sound quieting construction.

*A lush garden environnment with refreshing pool & relaxing sauna.

*Smooth access to Hwys. 8 & 5.

FROM $600

YOURNAME REALITY

(714) 555-7899

appropriate. White space will give your ad more prestige and help the reader notice your ad among other ads and even editorial space.

One developer featured mostly white space in his ad with a headline like: "Why Would You Pay $100,000 for Nothing?" The copy completed the picture by saying that his land was located in a prestigious and peaceful part of town — a perfect place to build a home.

You might also use white space following a headline like this:

Listed Below are
the Real Estate Offices
Offering More Service
than Linda Lipman Realty:

When you need someone who really cares,
call Linda Lipman Realty: 321-4000

A selective use of white space will help give your ads the feeling of distinction and help you to emphasize certain points in your copy.

The opposite of white space is black ink. You can increase the amount of ink in your ad by asking that your type be printed in reverse — white on black instead of black on white. Reverse type stands out if it's used as an accent. However, reading a big block of copy in reverse type is difficult, and generally should be avoided.

You should also check the newspaper's reverse printing quality before deciding to use reverse type in your ad. Often the ink runs over into the letters that were supposed to be clean white, especially if the type size is small or the type style is thin, ruining the effect you were trying to create. It's also important to find out how many other ads on the page have chosen reverse headlines, logos or copy since your aim is to make your ads stand out from the competition's.

One real estate firm started requesting that its logo be printed in reverse on the classified page. The logo definitely received more attention than those of the competing firms. So over the next few weeks, most of the brokers switched their logos to reverse. The end result was that the logos were all competing with each other again without any of them really standing out.

A screen has the effect of shading. Without colored ink, the shade is between black and white or gray. Screens come in percentages (ten percent, twenty percent and so forth) depending on how dark you want them.

Screening part or all of the ad is a good attention-getting device. Screens can also be used with colored ink. For example, if you're using royal blue for your headline type, you can have all or part of your ad on a light blue background by requesting a fifteen percent blue screen.

Borders have the same effect on ads as mats or frames have on paintings; they keep your eye from wandering out of the frame. Borders can be effective if they're not overused or in competition with the same border used in a lot of other ads. You can be sure that you have a distinctive border if you have an artist custom design one for you.

If you have a custom border, use it in all your ads. It will start building immediate visual recognition for your company, much the same way your logo does.

Emphasize Your "Signature"

You can also make a visual statement with your "signature" — company name, logo or slogan, in a display ad. Spend the time and money necessary to have a signature that you're proud of. Since it will be used in all of your display ads and other marketing materials, its cost over the years is minimal. Many salespeople, as well as brokers, are realizing the benefits of creating their own logos or slogans and using them in their own advertising.

Designing a display ad is a lot like arranging furniture. You start with an empty room and fill in your chairs, tables and accent pieces until you're comfortable. In advertising, you start with a blank space, and use copy as a starting point. Then you add the other design elements until you're comfortable. The newspaper should be able to supply you with a layout sheet. You can use this to help you visualize your space and how the elements will fit together.

Layout Hints

Your Placement Strategy

Besides design and position on the page, there's another factor that will determine how many readers notice your ads: where the ads are placed. The media buying department in an ad agency determines where to place the ad to get the kind of attention the advertiser is looking for.

Media questions include: Which publication has the right demographics? Which section of the newspaper attracts the right type of reader? On what day of the week (for a daily) should the ad be placed?

While these are all extremely important questions, you can probably find the answers yourself by calling the various media representatives in your area and asking them for a presentation and media kit. It will give you the circulation, income levels and family size of the readers, how much time each reader spends with the publication and so forth.

Since there are usually only a handful of local papers for a particular suburb or section of the city, you could try them all to see which newspaper creates the most feedback, even if the media kits all sound the same.

Which Section?

When you're placing classified ads, you know where your ad will appear. But you have a choice when you go the display route. The most logical location for a real estate ad in a major metropolitan daily is the Sunday Homes or Real Estate section. Sunday also generally has the highest circulation and most readers spend more time with their Sunday paper than with any other day's edition. Home buyers also regularly turn to the Homes section. However, because of all the competing ads, getting your ad to stand out among the bunch in this section is difficult. This is akin to the pros and cons of locating a retail business in a shopping center. The center attracts more shoppers than a stand-alone store in its own building. But many of the stores in the center are in competition with each other for the same shoppers.

Placing your ad in another section of the paper outside of the Real Estate section eliminates the competition problem, but the number of serious home buyers reading your ad will be reduced as well. You may want to try different sections of the paper (sports, features, TV listings).

Different sections may have different rates, but don't choose by price alone. Test the section by running your ad there for three weeks with an offer (free coloring books, miniature Christmas trees at holiday time, etc.) to judge response.

If you get a good response, try running a standard institutional ad (using ideas from the section on image-building ads) for three weeks and see if you get any comments or response. Then you'll know if your ad is truly getting noticed, or if just your free offer was attracting all the attention.

If you can advertise in the same position every week, readers will get used to looking for your ads there and your ad will become part of that page's or section's typical content. Then readers will expect to see your ads the same way they expect to see their favorite columnist or the comics in the same place. To give you an idea of how important position consistency is, editors know that if they change editorial positions at random, readers will protest immediately. If you try different positions all the time, nobody will know where to find you.

Another way of advertising in the local paper is to place a separate insert (like a flier or newsletter) in the publication. The flier could be either institutional or designed to advertise listings.

The advertiser pays for designing and printing the insert on his own. Then he pays the newspaper just for distribution based on the circulation. This rate is lower than advertising in the newspaper and allows you to print a full-page, four-color ad on glossy paper for insertion, rather than settling for black-and-white on newsprint.

Which Local Paper?

Local community newspapers can be tested easily. Don't think just because one newspaper is more popular or well known than another, it's the only place to advertise. One local newspaper may be the tops for news, but the other second-rate paper may pull better for advertisers because the readers are bored with the news or editorial sections and spend most of their time with the paper reading the ads. The same is also true for some of the prestigious national business publications. You may think such a publication is needed to attract readers for an ad for an expensive listing or commercial property. But in reality, many advertisers have found that people are more interested in reading the articles in those publications, rather than the ads.

The greatest portion of the real estate broker's or salesperson's advertising is done in newspapers. But local magazines are a smart choice for advertising more unusual properties or for placing some of your institutional ads. Even national magazines like *Time*, offer regional pages to advertisers in many parts of the country at prices that some large real estate offices can afford.

Other Publications

The prestige of having your ad in *Time* can set your office apart from the pack that advertises in the classified pages. But you need to measure the pulling power of these magazines for your message. Many local businesses say frankly that they didn't expect a response from their ad but use it to show their customers. Brokers or salespeople could use these ads in listing presentations to impress potential sellers.

Regional magazines often have a special advertising section for expensive homes and specialized magazines, like *Horses*, may be a logical place to attract buyers for horse properties. The special-interest magazine, rather than the newspaper, offers the advertiser the most direct target market.

Black-and-white or color photographs usually reproduce better in slick magazines, too. But if they come out monthly, they probably have at least a one-month lead time for advertisers which makes them a bad choice for advertising a single property. The property may be sold by the time the ad comes out.

For most real estate needs, the local newspaper is still the best buy. People prefer working with a local broker or sales associate when buying or selling a home. Therefore, even advertising in a magazine like *San Diego Home / Garden*, which is a high-quality local magazine covering the San Diego metropolitan area, may not be local enough for someone looking for a real estate professional right in his or her own neighborhood.

"Homes" magazines are another publication category that usually feature listing ads (with photos) from a metropolitan area. Very few articles are included. Since the ads are for listings exclusively, you can judge the effectiveness of these publications rather easily.

Test the magazine by advertising some listings in it and don't advertise these listings in the newspaper. If you get calls, your ad is a success. These magazines are offered free at grocery stores and a few local retail outlets. Shoppers, on the other hand, are mailed to everyone on a list whether they want them or not.

You will undoubtedly be asked to advertise in dozens of other publications and by many local organizations that publish newsletters or annual publications. Consider any investment in these as part of your community relations program, if you choose to participate.

Throw-aways and Shoppers

These publications are attractive to advertisers because they are mailed to every address in a restricted geographic area. That means they have a much higher circulation than the subscriber newspapers in the same area. They're also an effective and inexpensive way to reach people who don't read regular newspapers at all.

You can test the Shoppers by advertising a bargain listing. A headline like "No Qualifying" or "Cheaper Than Rent" would appeal to the readers who look through the Shoppers for garage sales and other bargain merchandise.

Another idea for advertising a low-priced property is to feature the monthly payment rather than the price in the headline: "$695 a Month." Many people are more concerned about their monthly housing payment than the price of the new home.

The monthly payment headline immediately lets people know if they can afford the house. But be sure that you are following Truth in Lending guidelines regarding full disclosure about financing by also including the full price, APR and terms, etc. in the body copy of the ad.

While Shoppers are an inexpensive way to

reach many people, don't rely on them as your exclusive advertising medium. Serious home buyers read their newspaper's classifieds regularly.

A Review and Comparison of the Media

In *Real Estate in the Eighties: A Study of Home Buyers and Sellers*, published in 1984 by the Newspaper Advertising Bureau, Inc. of New York, 67 percent of home buyers and sellers said they saw real estate advertising in newspapers. But 47 percent recalled seeing real estate ads on television, 26 percent heard it on radio, and 11 percent saw the ads in magazines. Yard signs accounted for 9 percent, billboards 8 percent, the *Pennysaver* 3 percent, direct mail 2 percent, and "all other" and "no answer" 4 percent.

In the same report, 67 percent of the buyers and sellers said they still checked the homes for sale in the classified section of the newspaper even after listing their home with a real estate brokerage or while having a broker show them homes to buy.

So you can see that newspapers are still the most popular source for advertising with brokers and the clients they hope to attract. This pattern is so clearly established, that no significant change is expected in the near future.

5.
Your Image Deserves It — Some Ideas for Your Institutional Advertising

Aside from classified and display ads for your listings, consider advertising to increase and improve your image. Marketing professionals call this institutional advertising.

Along with other marketing programs, institutional advertising could be crucial if you're trying to get established as a new brokerage or sales associate in your community. However, once your ads start getting noticed on a regular basis, people will think you've always been there.

Many brokers are hesitant about starting an image building campaign for two reasons. First, they can't really measure immediate results as easily as they can when they place an ad for an open house in the classified section.

Second, display advertising creates an additional expense. But it, along with other marketing and farming efforts, can be the distinguishing mark you create for yourself. The sooner you do that, the sooner you'll give clients a reason to use your services.

Distinguish Yourself

But what are you going to promote about yourself? What's your image? Most real estate offices and salespeople offer similar services — selling or listing homes.

Since many brokerages belong to a Multiple Listing Service (MLS), they all have access to the same inventory — listings. That leads many people to believe that all real estate brokerages and their salespeople are the same. This is probably the biggest obstacle you have to overcome in promoting your image in advertising. Just saying that you can sell homes or that you know financing, isn't enough to distinguish yourself from the competition.

But the majority of the institutional ads done by salespeople say just that. Their ads give the reader no compelling reason to pick up the phone and call.

Consider positioning your services to fit a certain market. To create a market for yourself, use the same procedure you use to decide on the probable market for a listing. Once you have identified a certain niche for yourself, you can start writing ads for that market. Using this narrow marketing approach rather than using a broad appeal is very effective. It makes you stand apart from your competitors.

Think about soap or toothpaste advertising. While various brands of soap products basically serve the same purposes, the manufacturers have distinguished themselves as the complexion bar or the deodorant soap, depending on the market they are trying to reach.

Toothpastes either appeal to the physical need to fight cavities or the emotional desire for a whiter smile. Although one toothpaste can probably do both, each one strives for a different appeal and market.

As a real estate professional, you know that you can sell property to anyone. But you also know that you're facing competition for every listing. If you're the only real estate agent in town advertising that you're the first-time buyer specialist or the veterans' agent, however, you may find that much of your competition is eliminated.

Many business owners believe that a listing in the Yellow Pages is a must. Some towns have the "big" book along with a dozen or more smaller directories and blue books, either aimed at the entire community or smaller special interest groups — like the Women's Yellow Pages, the Businessman's Yellow Pages and the Chamber of Commerce Directory. Institutional ads are the obvious way to go. But a few directories can absorb a broker's entire institutional budget for

Directories and Yellow Pages

the year!

While only one of your ads is set and printed in the directory, you may end up paying for that ad monthly, rather than just one time. Review the demographics for each directory carefully and compare these to the cost for the ad. Also, check to see how much overlapping of circulation the directories have. Are the same people getting the Yellow Pages, the Blue Book and the Chamber Directory? Are the recipients going to use all three? Which is the most popular in your community?

Focus on a Market by Using Testimonials

In real estate, many of your clients are:

- newlyweds
- empty-nesters
- families
- investors
- first-time buyers
- trade-up buyers

Try designing ads that appeal to each of these groups or other groups that include many of your clients and write ads for the markets you hope to break into.

One of the best ways to build credibility in a market is through a testimonial or referral statement from a client that belongs to the group you're trying to target.

Product research has shown that these statements are more credible than general claims the manufacturer makes to the public. Testimonials also help you appeal directly to others in the same situation as the one depicted in the ad.

Testimonials are particularly appropriate for real estate advertising because:

1. Most clients prefer using a brokerage or agent that has been recommended by someone they know rather than picking one out of the Yellow Pages.

2. Real estate is such a substantial investment that most people prefer working with someone they can trust. Building trust into your testimonial or other institutional message will increase its effectiveness.

3. Despite their effectiveness, testimonials are rarely used in ads by brokers and salespeople, so using them in your ads will really distinguish you from the competition.

Before you get started on a testimonial ad, here are a few suggestions:

- It must be believable.

- You must get a signed release form from your sources allowing you to use their names, photographs and statements in your ads.

• You can make your entire ad a testimonial, with lots of copy, if it holds the reader's interest and hits him emotionally.

You can also use testimonial-type ads to feature an anonymous client of yours. For example, if you're trying to attract first-time buyers, you should feature some first-timer in the ad. Be sure to use a photo of you with your clients.

Following are two examples of this type of testimonial:

**We Were Afraid to Turn in Our
Rent Receipts
But We're Happy We Did**

We wanted the security and tax benefits of home ownership, but we didn't think we could afford it. And after renting for years, we were a little worried about signing mortgage papers.

But Linda Lipman showed us that with low interest rates and tax deductions we hadn't had before, home ownership was not only easier than we thought, but more enjoyable.

Linda was with us every step of the way from house hunting to closing. Now we have a home of our own, an investment that keeps increasing in value, instead of a collection of rent receipts.

Linda showed us everything we needed to know. If you're a first-time buyer, call Linda Lipman today. Our no-obligation qualifying program will let you know how much home you can afford, so you can buy a home with confidence.

Linda Lipman Real Estate
444-3200

Investing in Real Estate Is Helping Us Enjoy a Profitable Retirement

There aren't many investments that beat real estate for tax benefits, capital appreciation and yes, income. The type of income that can turn an uncertain retirement into a worry-free future.

"Linda Lipman showed us how we could buy a small house — something we could afford and maintain ourselves — and rent it out to cover our mortgage payments. Over the years, the rent has increased and now it gives us the extra income we wanted in our Golden Years. Sometimes we don't know what we'd do without that rental house."

Linda can show you, too, how to accomplish your investment dreams with real estate. Call today: 444-3200.

Celebrity or Expert Testimonials

If you're lucky enough to have sold a celebrity's or expert's property, contact them for a testimonial. The celebrity might be a true superstar like the top player for your city's professional football team or just a local personality like a television talk-show host who is easily identified and well-liked by the community.

An expert, on the other hand, is someone like a real estate attorney, mortgage banker or sophisticated real estate investor. Your public will assume that these experts would only turn to a top-notch professional for real estate services.

This type of testimonial could be just the message you need to convince buyers of your expertise. Here's an example:

> "I know a lot about property law, but not much about home values...
>
> "As a real estate attorney, I help buyers and sellers with their closings almost every day and I know most of the real estate brokers in town. But I didn't know what my own home was worth, not really. That's why I'm glad I contacted Linda Lipman. She gave me an accurate market analysis of homes in my area before I listed. I knew what to expect every step of the way, not only at the closing."
>
> When real estate experts sell, they choose Linda Lipman. Shouldn't you?
>
> For a free market analysis before you sell, call 444-3200.

Another kind of testimonial you should consider is to advertise your buyers or sellers, rather than the properties themselves. To do this, first prepare a brief list of buyers and sellers you are working with now or who you've worked with in the past — single professionals, newlyweds, empty-nesters, young families. You can use them all or select just a few for the ad.

People reading the ad will most likely identify with one of the groups mentioned and your credibility will improve with that group. Here are two examples of ads written to attract buyers and sellers:

Advertise Your Buyers and Sellers for a Change

Linda Lipman Real Estate is happy to be helping your neighbors realize their dream homes:
Some of our recent clients:

• a new North Side doctor who has a very lucrative future, but no money for a down payment now

• a young, but growing family who needed a backyard their condo didn't have so their children could enjoy more outdoor playtime, under the safe supervision of a busy mom

• an active retired couple who wanted to spend more time with each other instead of maintaining their large home of 30 years

If you're looking for your dream home, call today.

Linda Lipman Real Estate has helped your neighbors sell their homes quickly. Ask:

• the family in the Willow Walk development. Their new home was ready for them, but they hadn't sold their lovely two-story until they contacted us.

• the senior citizens on Arlington Drive. They wanted to move in with their daughter in California before winter set in. They called us and started packing in October.

• the young family in one of our area's best located condos. They needed to be in their new home, close to school, before September. We sold their condo before they left for summer vacation and they had a wonderful time.

If you need to sell in a hurry, call us today.

All of these mini case histories appeal to a buyer's or seller's needs and emotions and those are the kinds of messages that are going to sell more homes.

Many of the approaches that are effective for writing classified ads for properties also work for institutional display ads. Selling *benefits* rather than *features* is again the key to this kind of advertising.

But instead of translating all the features of your listings into benefits for the buyers, you'll be listing all the features of your firm or all the attributes of your experience (if you're a sales associate) and translating those into benefits that would be meaningful to a buyer or seller.

Start with a worksheet of your accomplishments or the characteristics of your firm. Keep in mind the market that would be attracted by them. Your worksheet might look something like this:

Think Benefits Versus Features Again

Features	Benefits
Relocation Department	We can help you find a home anywhere you're going. We can sell your home to buyers from outside the area.
Annual Sales Over $20 Million	We not only list, we sell. We're successful.

15 Years of Experience	We've weathered good and bad. We'll sell your house regardless of market conditions.
Big Office	We have lots of agents working for you.
Small Office	We give you personal attention.

Some of your personal "features" can also be combined in each ad, but make sure you translate them into benefits. Compare the two ads following:

See Linda Lipman for All Your Real Estate Needs

- 9 years of experience
- attorney
- member of relocation service

*(Company
Name
Phone Number
Photograph)*

Buying or Selling A Home?
See Linda Lipman
For All Your Real Estate Needs

• For nine consecutive years, I've sold more than 40 houses a year — some of them just like yours.

• As an attorney, I have the legal background to help you understand every aspect of your sale.

• Our relocation service will find you a new house — wherever you're going. We also have access to out-of-town buyers who are moving into the area every day.

(Company
Name
Phone Number
Photograph)

The second ad is more effective for two reasons. First, it sells benefits rather than features. Second, it talks directly to the readers by addressing them as "you" rather than as an anonymous group. This is very effective in relating your message directly to your targeted audience.

Some of the most successful institutional ads offer free information. For example, your ad can offer free information on "How to Prepare Your

Provide Free Information

111

Home for Sale," "How to Choose a Real Estate Professional," "Little Known Ways to Finance a Home Purchase," or "Ten Mistakes to Avoid in Selling Your Home." Briefly outline some of the information you're offering and then encourage the reader to write or call for the entire brochure or pamphlet. It's easy to analyze the ad's results if you feature a coupon the reader returns for the information.

To increase your exposure, you should also prepare a press release announcing that you have free information available and where to call to request it. The newspapers often run these press releases as articles which are published at no charge.

To increase the chances of your press release being used, write it so that it reads like an article instead of an advertisement. (Chapter 8, "Get More Out of Your Media With Public Relations," includes more detailed information on preparing press releases.) A sample ad and press release offering free information follow:

Sample Ad

The Home-Selling Tip Book: Don't Make a Move Without It

Did you know that painting your home before selling it can return to you more than its cost, but wallpapering can make your house harder to sell?

These are some of the more than two dozen ideas that work to make your home sell in less time and at a higher price. These tips are yours in our unique Home-Selling Tip Book, written just for home sellers in our area. Send off the coupon below or stop in our office today for your free copy.

You'll be glad you did.

For: Immediate Release
From: Linda Lipman Real Estate
Contact: Linda Lipman
       321-3224
Date: January 1, 1999

Sample Press Release

**New Home-Selling Tip Book
Now Available**

Just in time for the busiest home selling season of the year, a new booklet listing tips for the home seller is now available.

"We noticed many of our sellers making a number of mistakes before listing their homes for sale. These mistakes cost them money or increased the length of time their houses needed to be on the market," said Linda Lipman of Linda Lipman Real Estate in Anaheim. "So we decided to publish our own booklet especially for this area. Now homeowners will know exactly what type of improvements will be the most cost efficient."

Some tips from the booklet include:

— If you're going to paint, choose light neutral colors.

— You can spend several hundred dollars removing overgrown trees and shrubs crowding the front yard and get a return of several thousand dollars in a higher sales price.

— Putting a drop of vanilla flavoring on a cool light bulb in one of your fixtures will let off a pleasant aroma when the lights are turned on later during a house showing.

— Be sure to disclose all known defects to your real

estate agent and buyer. In most cases, putting everything in your home in good working order will result in a quicker sale at a higher price.

You may get a free copy of the booklet by calling 321-3224 or visiting Linda Lipman Real Estate at 1221 W. Anaheim Rd., Anaheim.

- end -

If something looks and sounds newsworthy, it will have a higher readership and recall than the ho-hum or mundane. Which of these lead sentences grabs your attention? "Spring is home-buying season." "This spring, more than 10,000 Glendale residents will become homeowners for the first time, according to a just released home-buying study."

How do you get news into your ads? Announce company events or comment on real estate trends already in the news. For examples:

Linda Lipman Real Estate
Sells 1,000th House!

Thank you, Kenilworth. We've just sold our 1,000th house. We

News- worthy Ads

115

reached this milestone through good service and dedication to our business. But we couldn't have done it without you. When you're thinking of buying or selling, call us. One thousand of your neighbors already have.

Linda Lipman Real Estate
444-3200

Home Prices Are Up!

Just read the headlines. Home prices are headed higher. Your home is probably worth more today than it's ever been. But interest rates could be headed up later this year. That means there's no time like the present when it comes to selling your home. If you're thinking about making a move, you'll need all your home equity.

Call today for a no-obligation analysis of what your home is worth in today's market. You'll be surprised.

Linda Lipman Real Estate
444-3200

Notice how the first ad capitalizes on company news, while the second comments on events already in the newspapers. If you have news, don't bury it in the ad copy. Announce it in the headline. Do the same in your classifieds or display ads for listings.

Another tip is to advertise a Home of the Week (in either classified or display). This shows the home will be featured this week only (make sure it is) and adds that extra news element to your ad.

"Fuzzy" doesn't mean unclear in advertising. It means that warm feeling that brings a tear to your eye when you see the grandmother talking on the phone to her only grandchild on a long-distance telephone TV commercial. There are dozens of fuzzy ads you can create for your real estate firm — telling the kinds of stories that will give your potential clients a warm feeling about your firm.

Remember, all real estate brokerages offer similar services and products. The difference comes in the positioning and image. An example follows:

The Fuzzy Ad

It Looked Like They Wouldn't Get
Their New House

The sellers were miles away on a fishing trip. But Joe and Jan were here for just a short house-hunting trip, when they found the perfect place. We couldn't reach the sellers by phone, but we could get there by car. So that's what we did. We drove up to the mountains to present Joe and Jan's offer. They needed to know before they left the city and we got them their answer. Here they are today in their new home.

Photo

When you need conventional answers in an unconventional way, call:

Linda Lipman Real Estate
321-4400

We Roll Up Our Sleeves

The buyers wouldn't sign the closing papers until they were sure the previous renters were out of their new house. But the renters couldn't find affordable movers on short notice. It was a choice between a delayed closing and rolling up our sleeves and going to work. We found the first choice unacceptable to our buyers who we knew deserved better.

The second choice was a little inconvenient, but we knew we could do it. So that Sunday, while most other real estate brokers were holding open houses or taking the day off, we helped move the renters out of the buyers' new house. On Monday, the house was theirs and ready for them to call home.

When you need a real estate professional who's more than just a salesperson, call:

**Linda Lipman Real Estate
We Find a Way
321-4400**

Can you see how these fuzzy ads build emotion and involve the reader in the story? One important note: be sure the fuzzy stories you tell are true.

Create a Series

Just as display advertising should be placed consistently, your message (if it's a good one) should be repeated, too. It doesn't always have to be the same message, however. It can be part of a series. For example, one successful advertising campaign for a new home builder asked a separate question in each ad. The questions really were written just to intrigue the reader and involve him in thinking about answers. Questions similar to those used in the campaign follow:

What has 40 kitchens, 85 bath rooms and $75,000 worth of landscaping?

> What has a 250-acre lake and 12 tennis courts?

> What has 60 fireplaces and more than 1,000 rooms?

These questions were featured in large type in separate display ads throughout the newspaper (which was a large, metropolitan daily). The rest of each ad said, "For the answer, see the (name of the builder) ad in the Homes & Garden Section." The ad in the Homes section read like this:

> What has 40 kitchens, 85 bath rooms, $75,000 worth of landscaping, a 250-acre lake, 12 tennis courts, 60 fireplaces and more than 1,000 rooms?
>
> Lipman Homes' new Willow Walk neighborhood in Bartlett.

The body copy of the ad went on to describe the homes in more detail and offered directions to the development. The ad series was very successful for the developer and all the homes were sold at the grand opening. These ads could easily be adapted to a real estate firm by asking questions that feature all the homes a company has listed or all the sales associates of the firm. Examples follow:

Who has 140 years of real estate experience?

Who has sold more than 3,000 homes?

Who spent more than $100,000 on gifts to home sellers and buyers?

The answer, of course, is your firm. Obviously, other questions that are more appropriate or accurate may be substituted. You can use each ad in the series throughout the newspaper as this one was, or on consecutive Sundays or other days you normally advertise. For local papers, this may be every Thursday, the only day the paper comes out. Another way to use a series is to feature popular misconceptions and use the ad to change those myths. Each ad in your series can feature one myth in the headline.

Examples follow:

The Home Buyer's At-Home Test

(True or False) You need a lot of money to buy your first house.

Answer: More than 25 percent of all homes available for sale in the Multiple Listing Service for this area can be bought with less than a $4,000 down payment.

The Home Buyer's At Home Test

(True or False) It will cost you money to find your first home by using the services of a real estate broker.

Answer: If you buy any home from Linda Lipman, you will not be charged any fee for services like prequalifying for a loan, previewing homes for your inspection, explaining purchase agreements, finding an escrow company and lender, and many other important services.

This has been another in the Home Buyer's At-Home Test series, sponsored by Linda Lipman Real Estate. For a copy of this complete home-buying information kit, please call 321-4400.

Plan on Institutional Ads for the Long Haul

Before you embark on designing display ads for your institutional messages, realize that this will be a continuing cost. Classifieds can be used on occasion — just to advertise certain types of listings, but one display ad to improve your image loses all of its potential if the message isn't continued over time. How has McDonald's become so well known? By advertising regularly.

And why did 87 percent of Americans in a 1985 Gallup survey say that they had heard of

Century 21? Century 21 spent $31 million on advertising that year. What do you think the survey results would have been if the successful real estate franchise organization had advertised only once that year? Aside from building a high profile among the public, Century 21 brokers and salespeople are quick to mention their company's visibility as a prime advantage of putting on the gold jacket.

If you advertise just once, you can't accurately judge the ad's effectiveness and you've lost all the money you put into your ad. The first step to planning your institutional strategy is to find out the advertising costs, the various ad sizes available and then set your own budget.

You may not be ready for $31 million worth of television commercials in prime time. But your goal is consistency and continuity. If you can't afford a regular schedule of full-page ads, substitute two-column ads monthly rather than a full-page position at random.

Plan a year in advance. In fact, most newspapers offer a discount for buying on a schedule or certain lineage volume over time. Of course, be prepared to change the schedule if market conditions or opportunities warrant.

Deciding on an image or message for your ads is the hard part. This section has offered several approaches, including featuring your benefits, focusing on a market, using testimonials, providing information, highlighting news, promoting the warm and fuzzy feeling and using an integrated series.

You can adapt any of these to suit your image and market. As real estate becomes increasingly competitive, the broker who doesn't think beyond classifieds will be left behind.

6.
Enhance Your Advertising with Brochures and Fliers

N ow that you're more comfortable working with the media — both press releases and advertising — start looking for more marketing opportunities outside of the mass media. Preparing brochures and fliers to complement your media program is the most likely choice.

Your promotional literature helps you establish more credibility for your company, yourself and your inventory. How many times have you tried to tell a client about a listing or your services and received this response: "Do you have anything in writing?" How many buyers visit open houses, later to think: "Which house had the pool? Where was the house with the weeping willow trees?"

Brochures and fliers can fill a variety of

gaps in your marketing/communications program. Some ideas for brochures include:

- One on your firm or your services and experience (if you're a sales associate)

- One directed at recruiting new sales associates

- One directed at soliciting new listings

- Informative brochures on topics like financing, how to get your home ready for sale and the condominium lifestyle

- Specific property brochures where the listing warrants it

Fliers can be distributed in your farm area to announce special promotions, like a drawing for a Christmas tree or they can serve as quick sales pieces on listings. Some ideas for distributing fliers include:

- Keep them at the listing for distribution to both sales associates and their clients

- Give them to buyers visiting an open house

- Mail them to clients and neighbors before an open house

- Distribute them weekly to sales associates in other offices

Good brochures and fliers depend on the same copywriting and design techniques that are common to good advertising. But with advertising, you rely on the newspaper for printing and circulation. With brochures and fliers, you'll need to address these areas as well.

Many individuals think they need a brochure but then they don't know who should have it. Others spend money hiring professionals to handle the writing and design, but then print their piece on white bond paper using an in-house copy machine. If your circulation or distribution isn't targeted well or your printing is amateurish, your campaign will fail.

The chief advantage of a brochure or flier for a listing is the opportunity to say or show more about the property because you have more space for the message than the typical ad offers. If you can't afford a full-page ad for a listing, you could look into a full-page flier that is either hand-delivered or mailed to your market.

Another advantage — and one that shouldn't be overlooked — is the ability to offer the piece to a select audience. For example, you could use a one-page flier to advertise your listings to sales

Targeting Your Audience

associates in your area. You know that typical media advertising doesn't usually produce sales of the advertised listings. But other agents from your own office or other brokerages can and do participate in co-op sales.

Consider that hundreds of listings may be available to sell from the Multiple Listing Service books and on-line systems. Most areas have at least a six-month supply of resale inventory. If you're an agent who concentrates on listings, you need other agents to sell your homes. How can you make your listings stand out in the computer or the listing books to other salespeople?

One way is the weekly flier. This flier can be used to advertise all your listings, not just the ones taken that week. Since many agents use fliers, you will need to make yours stand out from the pile already in circulation.

Make your flier "newsy." In other words, don't just use the same advertisements for your listings every week. Sales associates may get tired of seeing the same properties highlighted in the same way. Try to mention some new angle on the listing each time you offer it in the flier. For example, the first flier ad might say:

JUST LISTED
EXECUTIVE RANCH

This is one of Fort Lee's most admired and desirable homes in our most exclusive neighborhood. Your clients will enjoy outdoor activities in the park-like manicured grounds. The discriminating buyer will find only the finest workmanship and construction in this spacious custom-designed home. New light-colored wallcoverings decorate the four bedrooms and three baths. The kitchen features a skylighted breakfast area for family dining and an expansive wall of oak cabinets for storage. Of course, there's a formal living and dining room, and you'll also see an extra bonus room for sewing, crafts, hobbies or study.

The perfect family home at $327,000. Home is vacant and on lock box.

Note: Please don't let dog out of laundry room.

Preview today and show tonight, your buyers will love you!

The next time you advertise:

PRESTIGIOUS LIVING
IN HIGHLAND VALLEY

Single-level — perfect for any client — especially one who desires an address that matches his success. From the tall trees outside to the custom cabinets in the kitchen, there are just too many custom features to list. But now with BRAND-NEW carpeting and a $2,000 allowance toward closing costs for your buyer! Four bedrooms and three baths with 20- x 24-foot bonus room. Highly motivated seller has bought another home. Will consider all offers! This home offers the best of both worlds — high class living and a low budget price: $327,000. Show today before it's sold!

Notice that the second ad has been updated with some new information about the listing. If you build a reputation for newsy ads, other agents will be more likely to read your fliers.

By distributing the flier only to agents, you can promote the listing in different ways to make it exciting to show and sell. You can also make your distribution even smaller, but more productive, by initially offering the flier to a select group of agents — the top selling agents in your area, of course. They'll want to read your fliers if they know that you are distributing them several days ahead of schedule to top agents only. Try it and see if you don't hear from more agents about your listings.

Another good idea is to hand deliver the flier yourself. As you know, there's no better technique for selling than person-to-person contact. By calling on other agents, you start building rapport with selling agents, who may be able to sell your next listing.

You can also create another flier for an audience of specific buyers. For example, for this $327,000 listing, you could design a flier and mail it to owners of homes in the $200,000-$250,000 range. This is the most likely bracket of buyers who could afford your listing and may be interested in trading up.

You could produce the mailing list yourself by knowing what neighborhoods in your area fall into that value range, or you could contact a mailing list broker. These mail houses are listed in the Yellow Pages. By using a flier, rather than a newspaper ad, you could direct your communication specifically toward this audience. For example:

READY TO TRADE UP TO A NEW HOME?

Look no further. You can afford executive living. The seller of this exclusive ranch-style family home will help pay your closing costs! And new carpeting already has been added — another savings for you! If you're looking for four double-sized bedrooms and three custom baths with the most prestigious address in the community, it's time to start packing. Bonus room is perfect for extra guests, library, hobbies or entertainment room. Manicured lot for easy care and custom features like skylights and island in kitchen.

**ALL THIS IN HIGHLAND VALLEY
FOR $327,000.**

Call for more information and all the financing details.

Another select audience for your flier could be nearby homeowners. In this case, you might use a flier to announce an open house in the neighborhood. Again, you could direct the writing just to this group. Example:

**JUST LISTED, RIGHT HERE
IN HIGHLAND VALLEY
WILL BE FEATURED IN AN OPEN HOUSE
THIS WEEKEND**

Come see this delightful ranch this weekend. It's roomier than most homes in the area — with four bedrooms, three baths and bonus room! Custom features inside include skylights, real oak paneling, granite kitchen counters, spa-jetted bathtub in luxurious master bedroom suite. Brand-new carpeting and wood floors in family room and kitchen. If you'd like to stay in the area, but are looking for more room and more upgrades, this is the home for you. Or maybe one of your friends or family members have always said how much they like the neighborhood. Here's their chance to become one of your neighbors!

1234 Oakwood Drive
Offered at $327,000
Open noon to 4 p.m. Sunday, March 3

By deciding on a market for the listing and your flier, you can use different appeals in your headlines. If you just want to reach everyone that you normally would with a newspaper ad, do just that. Contact your local paper and see if they'll stuff your flier in the paper before it's delivered.

Do You Need a Flier or a Brochure?

A flier is supposed to look newsy — as if it's just been produced for some important event. It serves a different purpose than a brochure, which should look more substantial to either match the quality of the property being offered or to last longer in a client's file.

Since the flier can be produced for much less cost on much cheaper paper than a full-blown professionally designed brochure, you might want to try producing some fliers before you commit yourself to the cost of the brochure. Or you could send out fliers first, saving the brochures for your hottest prospects after they've responded to your flier.

The difference between a flier and a brochure is like the difference between a newsletter and a magazine. Not everyone saves newsletters, but binders containing magazines from 20 years ago are not uncommon.

With that in mind, you can write the flier like a newspaper, knowing that another "edition" will be out shortly. But the copy for the brochure should be timeless. Don't say, "Interest rates are expected to remain low this summer." What happens if you still want to use your brochure in December? Instead, use words like "recent" or "in the near future."

The Company or Sales Associate Brochure

Besides marketing your listings, you'll want to use a brochure to promote your company or yourself. A seller may interview three or more brokers and salespeople before deciding with whom to list his home.

When decision time comes, a seller may not remember which listing agent had the best presentation, had a relocation department or property management department. Which agent said he was a past president of the Chamber of Commerce? Who had a college degree? Who has been in real estate for ten years?

This is all information you could include in a brochure. Then be sure to leave it with your prospect, so he knows and remembers all your selling points. The brochure could have many other uses, such as direct mail, and could be a centerpiece of your institutional advertising.

So you think you need a brochure, but don't know what to put in it? Starting with an outline helps. Write down and number all your salient points, or write each point on an index card. Don't worry too much now about whether you're including unimportant points. You can edit your list or cards later.

If you use cards, you can reorganize them quickly and change the order of the information. Before you begin writing it's also important to determine who your audience will be and decide what approach you will use — folksy, sophisticated, etc.

Following are two rough outlines, the first for a brokerage brochure and the second for a sales associate brochure.

Writing The Brochure

Brokerage Brochure Outline

I. Introduction
  A. Describe your service
  B. Give your office location
    1. Tell what area you serve
  C. Describe your corporate struc-
     ture and affiliations
  D. Discuss the problems your office
     tries to solve for its clients
II. Qualifications of brokerage
  A. Number of years in business
  B. Description of departments
    1. Brief explanation of services
       they offer
  C. Organization memberships

135

   D. Ranking in relation to competitors

   E. Summaries of transactions company has handled

III. Testimonials

   A. Statements from related professionals you have worked with, such as mortgage bankers

IV. Staff

   A. Number of salespeople

     1. Areas they serve

   B. Personal and professional background of broker

V. Unique features

   A. Any guarantees you offer

   B. Special marketing tools

   C. Selling services

   D. Buying services

Sales Associate Brochure Outline

I. Qualifications

   A. Education

   B. Previous employment history

   C. Your title or licence held within the organization: vice president, manager, sales associate or broker

II. Past real estate experience

   A. Average annual number of sales

   B. Dollar volume of sales

   C. Year you started with brokerage
   D. Any positions held on Board of
      Realtors
   E. Areas of specialization
III. Community experience
   A. Years living in community
   B. Membership in community organi-
      zations
   C. Other civic and philanthropic
      activities
IV. Testimonials
   A. Summaries of different transac-
      tions
   B. Recommendations of previous
      clients
   C. Statements by community leaders
V. Unique services
   A. Buying services
   B. Selling services
   C. Summary of how you approach your
      work and what you will provide
   D. The quality of your service
      versus the competition

Your brochure should have a beginning, middle and end which is easy to accomplish when you start with an outline. The reader should be able to reach the logical conclusion that you are experienced, professional, competent and reliable. Strive for a personal tone and remember to stress the benefits and not only the features of your background and services.

How Do You Handle Production?

One of your biggest challenges will be the production and printing of your piece. When you place an ad, this area is usually handled by the newspaper or magazine, but you should be prepared to take over these responsibilities yourself when you produce brochures and fliers.

As in media advertising, your brochure copy will be typeset but either typesetting or typewriting is fine for the flier. If you are going to have your piece typeset, be sure to get estimates from several local typesetters. These businesses are usually competitive and you may be able to get a better price by shopping around.

If you're going to produce fliers and brochures regularly, you may want to buy a desktop publishing system for the office. With it you can produce typeset-like quality and graphics without using outside typesetters, artists and designers. You'll need a personal computer, appropriate software and laser printer to get the highest quality. These systems allow almost anyone to produce fliers, brochures, ads — even newsletters, newspapers, magazines or books — that nearly match professionally typeset materials.

However, you'll still need something intelligent to say (the computer can't put words together the way a top-notch copywriter can) and a flair for graphic design. If you go overboard in changing typefaces, adding rules and borders and have column widths that are difficult to read, your computer won't know, but your audience will.

After you (or your artist) have pasted up your copy, proofread it again to be sure that corrections have been made and that nothing has been left off in the paste-up process. Then start reviewing the entire piece, including the graphics to be sure that everything is where it is supposed to be.

Cost, quality and service are the three considerations in choosing a printer. First, see if you can get recommendations from associates who have used printers in the past. Also check with your Chamber of Commerce, the Yellow Pages, local shopping centers or business districts and the publishers of direct mail solicitations you have received. Since printing is a fairly competitive business, you'll probably be able to find several local printers.

Picking the Printer

Often, if your printer is right in the area, free delivery and pick-up are available. Before you choose one however, have the representative give you price quotes and some samples of jobs that are similar to yours.

When you receive the samples, look for broken type, ink that isn't dark enough, smears on the page or copy that seems to be falling off the page. If you find any of these problems, the printer won't be able to provide the quality you are looking for.

If everything looks good, meet the people who will be handling your account. Do they seem agreeable? Do they get back to you on a timely

139

basis to answer questions? When you visit their offices, do they seem organized and tidy or would they lose your order? Would you be treated like a big client, or shoved aside when a bigger job comes in? What is their policy if a client isn't happy with the completed job? Is the bulk of their business in brochures and fliers or books and catalogs?

Be prepared to tell the printer how many copies you need, the type and size of paper, color of ink, folding requirements, number of photographs, any other special graphic elements like reverses or screens and how soon you need your job. Then he'll be able to give you a bid, which you should get in writing.

Colored inks are slightly more expensive than black ink and using two colors (black and green, for example) is even more expensive since the press must be cleaned between each inking. Also try not to make any changes late in the printing process. These will be costly corrections.

Picking the Paper

If you're sure about your paper choice, order it at the printer several weeks in advance of your job. Sometimes ordering paper at the time you drop off your camera-ready copy will delay your finished product. You can get some help in choosing paper from your graphic designer (if you have one) or your printer.

For example, coated (glossy) paper is better for reproducing photos, but printing on coated paper takes longer to dry. Paper, like anything else, goes on sale. The printer may have access to paper that is on special at the time you bring in your order. So, ask the printer what papers might be discounted so you can take advantage of the savings.

Printing papers come in different textures, colors and weights. Twenty-four pound is a letterhead weight, and eighty pound is about the weight of a magazine cover. To a large extent, the feel and look of the paper will account for the finished quality of your piece. If you're going to be printing fliers every week, you should buy a year's supply of paper in advance. Like anything else, volume discounts are available. Buying 52,000 sheets at once will be cheaper than buying 1,000 sheets every week for 52 weeks.

Any brochure or flier should provide information and contribute to favorable image building. Before your piece goes on to production, be sure you have succeeded in those two areas. As with ad copy, stress the benefits and advantages of your company or listing. Don't let the brochure's recipients think: "Oh here's another sales piece on why I should buy real estate." Be sure your advantages really stand out.

While a brochure can never stand alone in the sales process, it can be an important tool in generating and qualifying new prospects, paving the way for you to make the sales.

Meet Your Objective

141

7.
Make Newsletters Part of Your Campaign

Although advertising, press releases, brochures and fliers can be an effective way to reach your target market, you should consider adding a regularly published newsletter to your campaign. Business, non-profit and special interest groups have used newsletters for years, because they know they are a unique and effective way to reach their target markets. Part brochure, part flier, a newsletter can improve your image in ways the other materials can't. Your newsletter can establish you as a community real estate resource — providing information on local market conditions, tips on home repair and improvement and even news from your company, such as awards recently won or new services added.

Unlike general circulation newspapers, newsletters continue to enjoy an ever expanding readership. It seems that while we don't have much time these days to read general interest publications that cover a variety of global topics that may or may not be of interest to us, we can still find the time to learn more about our professions, our hobbies or our communities by reading a newsletter.

Perhaps one reason why newsletters are so effective is because they use short articles to offer the reader information that is of interest to him. In addition, while all real estate offices advertise, very few produce a newsletter. There goes your competition!

A newsletter is a useful tool in any market. When sales are going well, there's much more competition too, so your newsletter can be your edge in this type of market. Naturally, you need to get your name out even more when sales are in a slump to start bringing in new business.

However, the newsletter is primarily a farming tool. Better than note pads and key chains, an informative publication can truly build your credibility as a real estate expert. Giving away ballpoint pens and refrigerator magnets is something that any carpet cleaning or other service company can do, but few of them can offer valuable information on home ownership. That is a slot that only you as the neighborhood real estate professional, can fill.

You can use your newsletter to communicate with homeowners in the subdivision that

Purpose of the Newsletter

comprises your farm area, past clients or even hopefuls — such as trade-up buyers. You also can send individual copies to clients on your referral list or use them as door-openers for FSBOs.

Don't forget to target your newsletter to buyers as well as potential sellers in your farm area. One way to do this is to include a separate flier stuffed in the newsletter with pictures and copy describing your listings.

National Newsletter Companies

If you don't want to go into the publication business, consider a national newsletter. Marketing and newsletter companies publish these and advertise them in real estate publications. These companies generally offer one or two newsletters to choose from and will send you samples. You then simply order the amount you need to cover your client list or farm area.

Several of the larger real estate firms offer a pre-printed newsletter to their salespeople in much the same way. These newsletters are usually exclusive to the company such as Coldwell Banker or Century 21. However, if your company offers a standard newsletter to its salespeople, it may not be tailored to address the concerns of your particular farm. But these newsletters can be imprinted with your name and photo or even folded and mailed for you.

Sound easy? Sure. And the cost is fairly reasonable too. These newsletters do offer you a way to reach your farm on a regular basis. In fact, when you know your order is coming in, it may give you the incentive to "get out there" and meet the homeowners you'll be giving the newsletter to. That's probably better than not farming at all. But think about the most successful and well-read newsletters. They are special-interest or locally oriented to a narrow market. Can a national newsletter do that successfully? Not really. Does a national newsletter company know that a park is being built right in a subdivision that you've been farming? Or that a new employer is coming to town and will bring hundreds of transferred executives looking for new homes?

Consider a newsletter that a Southern California sales associate was distributing. In it was information on how to keep your basement dry. Unfortunately, homes in Southern California don't have basements. Remember, the three most important considerations in buying real estate are location, location and location. In other words, buying a home in your town is different from buying property in Detroit.

In order for national newsletters to sell and be profitable, they must offer information that's pertinent to all areas of the country. However, in general, national newsletters don't reach your target market with any news that's of particular interest to them. Instead, they tend to rehash information that's already been distributed nationally and include a lot of fillers like recipes. Real estate salespeople have more to offer than that. So, a national newsletter should be your

145

second choice. First you should consider writing your own, even if it's short.

Should You Publish It Yourself?

You'd be surprised. Some of the best newsletters are produced by salespeople. After all, you know the market you're trying to reach and what you want to say. Newsletters (like many newspapers) are best if they reach a very defined market — local. If you can produce different newsletters, each for a different audience or subdivision, that's ideal. People are really interested in what is going on in their own neighborhood — how much their homes have increased in value, what the problems are with the homes or just information on their neighbors.

Thinking of what to say may not be much of a problem for you. But getting the newsletter out on schedule may be more of an obstacle. Some salespeople get the newsletter out once. But then, even though they have the best of intentions, the newsletter becomes a low priority compared to listing presentations, open houses, calling lenders, lawyers or escrow companies and general day-to-day real estate business. And so, after the first issue, the newsletter goes out of publication and the real estate agent starts to think it wasn't a very worthwhile project anyway because it didn't bring in any new listings. But, like farming, you must continue your newsletter over time to get your desired results. If you don't put in the time, you don't get the results.

146

As in all farming, to be successful, you must maintain regular contact. If your farm hears from you every other year, you're not going to be very effective. The same applies to the newsletter. Be sure you can produce it on schedule from the start.

It's also equally important to make sure that you can take the time to produce a professional and tasteful newsletter. If you aren't going to take the time to develop the content, check your spelling and grammar and have it attractively printed, your newsletter won't contribute to your image and may even detract from it. Then, your newsletter has failed.

Your Content

It's a good idea to include articles in your newsletter that aren't geared to just buyers and sellers. After all, most people reading the newsletter won't be in the real estate market right now. If you title every article, "Now is the Time to Sell Your Home" or something similar, your newsletter won't appeal to many homeowners. But do keep most of the information relative to home ownership and real estate investment. That way you'll still be left with a wide range of interesting topics to choose from without having to include fillers.

If you're ready to give newsletter writing a try, you'll need something to say. After you've decided how much you have to say, you can decide on how many pages to include in your newsletter and how often to publish it.

Start With a List

Just as you need a good outline when you plan a brochure, start with a list of possible article ideas when you're planning your newsletter. It's best to start out with more article ideas than you need and then use the strongest ones to produce your best possible newsletter. Here's a list to use as an example:

1. New Library Within Walking Distance of ABC Subdivision

2. Ways to Reduce Household Hazards During Fire Season

3. Free Want Ad Column for Community

4. Open House Schedule

5. Property Management Dept. Now Open

6. Q and A on Housing Finance

7. Calendar of Community Events

8. Home Improvement Tips

9. Elementary School Test Scores Ranked #1 in State

10. Homes Selling Faster Than Usual

11. Elementary School Test Scores

12. Home Improvement Tips

From this starting list, choose your best and most timely article ideas for your audience. Now rank these ideas in order of importance. As you rank the ideas, decide from which angle or point of view you're going to approach each story. Remember to keep your particular audience in mind when you do this. Ideally, you want to present each story so that it offers positive real estate information of particular importance to your chosen audience. Using the above as an example, you might wind up with a list like this:

1. New Library (angle on how it may affect home values)

2. Homes Selling Fast (angle on amount of appreciation)

3. Open House Schedule (featuring those in subdivision)

4. Property Management Department (angle on service)

5. Calendar of Community Events

6. Elementary School Test Scores

7. Home Improvement Tips

As you can see, all of the news stories ended up being used this time. However, you might want to drop some from your initial list if you find out that they're not of interest to your audience at the moment. On the other hand, you might want to make features like Home Improvement Tips, Finance Q and A, Trivia or Want Ads a regular part of your newsletter. If you're going to use a Want Ads section in every newsletter, however, make sure you always have room for it. If you solicit ads for a Want Ad column, be sure to use all the ads that are submitted.

Keep your articles balanced between newsworthy, educational, promotional and entertaining. And think of your audience first. Remember, you'll be communicating with people who have just moved to the area and those who have been there for years.

Coming up with ideas for articles is just as important as the writing itself but it doesn't make sense to have a well-written article on an irrelevant topic. So spend some time watching and reading the news in your community and get to know what people are interested in.

Article Placement

Just like a newspaper, your page one story should be the most dynamic piece you have. Your lead article on this page should definitely feature something newsy on the local residential market or local news affecting home values or the quality of life in the neighborhood.

Some community issues you might want to address in your page one feature stories are: What is the Average Amount of Time People Own Their Homes Here and Why, Your Neighborhood Developments, Type of Home Most Suited to First-Time Buyers in Your Area, Finding a Dream Home in Your Area, Our Schools — How They Help Make Our Neighborhood Attractive. This kind of local news is critical to building a readership for the publication.

Another idea for page one could be a news briefs column, each with identifying subheads to help break up the space and give the appearance of short, easy to read stories.

Page two articles may be more general real estate related material. One popular column (as is exemplified by the number of daily newspapers that feature this column) is a real estate question and answer column. With this format, you can cover a larger quantity of information and the reader can pick and choose the questions that appeal to him. Topics can range from financing, home construction, home buying and selling techniques and legal issues to landscaping questions. Or you could do a question and answer column on one topic specifically like home financing. You would write the questions and answers or request that your readers submit questions for the column to you.

Tax reform will continue to be a major source of confusion especially as the rules are still changing from the original legislation. The second article on page two could be a regular tax feature reminding home owners of their tax benefits and offering information on all the changes that come about. If you don't feel comfortable paraphrasing tax articles that have already appeared in publications (be sure you give the publication credit, such as "according to *Changing Times* magazine"), you could contact a local certified public accountant to write the short article for you. That way, you could fill the space easily and the accountant may gain a valuable public relations message to reach his audience.

Page three can be reserved as the company's advertising page for listings, complete with photos and descriptions of property for sale or it can be a regular feature on open houses scheduled for the next weekend. If you choose not to "advertise," alternative article topics include home improvement ideas, landscaping "corner" and real estate investment tips.

Page four is the back page. You may need to use part of it as space for the mailing label if that's your method of distribution. With the portion that's left, you may want to do a trivia column (extremely high readership), a company news column (stressing the services of your company) or a feature on a successful local real estate investor.

Charts usually have high readership, too. You might feature mortgage information; the amount of time the typical listing takes to sell; how to compute monthly payments based on loan amount, interest rate and term; or what various home remodeling projects cost and how much resale value they add to a home.

The main thing to remember when writing your articles is to put "news" in your newsletter. Because the newsletter more closely resembles a letter (if it's informal) or a newspaper (if it's typeset with display type headlines and pictures), your publication should be informative in nature rather than marketing oriented. If readers recognize it as a solely promotional vehicle, it will lose readership.

You should follow the same principle you used to determine your story line-up when you write your stories. Start your story with the most significant, timely and interesting information you have on the topic. Then add supporting details to your main story idea in the paragraphs that follow. Try to keep all your stories upbeat, stressing the value of home ownership or the quality of your service. You should also use a variety of story lengths.

Break up your information into short paragraphs and get right to the point in each. These are easiest to read. Don't get too hung up on comparing your newsletter writing to that of a professional's. Your message is the important key here. Just write simply and in a friendly style and chances are your grammar will take care of itself. Do proofread all your work, however, and make sure you correct all typos, spelling and factual errors. If you don't think you're

Writing Your Newsletter

153

capable of that, it's best to leave your newsletter to a professional. You want the publication to create an awareness and develop integrity for your business.

Just like ads, all your stories should have headlines. If the articles are long, include subheads as well. Needless to say at this point, make sure that any claims you make in your headlines are supported in the story's copy.

Design and Production

For a four-page newsletter (the most common size), try for two to three articles or elements per page. Elements include graphs, charts or material set off in a box or with another border around it. The newsletter combines several techniques from brochures and fliers. That means you'll be responsible for production and printing as well as copywriting and graphics as in media advertising. The newsletter is part flier in that you want it to look newsy — straight off the press with some information that must be read immediately. It's also part brochure because you don't want your newsletter to look amateurish or unprofessional in any way.

You will need a format — the size of the page, number of pages and number of columns on each page. A four-page newsletter is usually printed on an 11- x 17-inch sheet size folded in half. A two-page newsletter may be printed on both sides of an 8-1/2- x 11-inch sheet.

For either of these sizes, two or three columns are best. It's difficult to read one wide column that goes full-width across the entire page.

As in advertising, your newsletter should have the same appearance every time you publish it. If you want to redesign down the road, that's fine. But don't redesign each issue. Therefore, your first issue may take more time than the rest because you'll need to choose a type style, headline style and banner (or publication name).

Your banner can run across the top or along the side of the front page. Most real estate agents use about the top third to half page for the banner and some accompanying information that identifies themselves, their company name, address and phone number and even their photo. Give your newsletter a name that's different from your company name. Examples are Real Estate Trends, Homeowner News or Homes Today. You could use one of these names (or a variation) combined with the name of the subdivision or town to let people know this is their publication. You can put the name of your company under the name of the newsletter:

Willow Walk Homeowner News
the Newsletter of Jack Scott & Co. Realtors

Now you're ready to prepare a mock-up of what the newsletter will look like. This may add a little time to your first newsletter, but once you have a design established, you can reuse it over and over. The mock-up will help show you how long your articles should be and give you an idea what the publication will look like when it's finished. You can also take it to printers to get estimates.

You can either type your copy on a typewriter or word processing system with clean, dark ribbon or have your articles typeset. Typing your articles will give your publication a more informal look and that may be just what you're looking for. Typesetting will look more professional but will be more costly, of course, and will require more planning. If you decide to go this route, several salespeople in the office can get together and each write an article or two and then share the cost of the typesetting or even printing. For artwork, you can ask a graphics house to supply you with clip art. This is usually the most economical as well as professional in appearance.

In designing your pages, don't "butt" headlines. If you need to put two stories next to each other, put a box around one.

Simplicity is the key in design, just as it is in well-written articles. Easy to read pages will help you get your message across better than cluttered pages. Just as with advertising, white space is a design element. Leaving adequate (at least one-half inch) margins at the top, bottom and sides and between columns (at least one-quarter inch) is important. When you get to pages two and three of the four-page newsletter, look at them as a two-page spread. It is here you should plan your design so the pages are attractive when your reader looks at them together.

Here you will have to pay attention to balance and symmetry.

To draw attention to important stories or words, you could underline (sparingly) or use boldface or italic. Art supply stores stock sheets of "rub-off" type that you can use for headlines or symbols, like bullets, arrows or stars.

Your Distribution and Schedule

If you're using your newsletter to "advertise" yourself in your farm area to get more listings, door-to-door distribution is best. But you may want to mail the newsletter in your area or to some clients who aren't in your farm. Type these names onto mailing labels. If your list is rather substantial, a secretarial service can handle the labels for you.

You should be able to fold the newsletter into thirds and staple, stamp and label before mailing. If you've had your newsletter professionally printed (versus using a copy machine), you can order the newsletters already folded from the printer. Discuss the project with your printer so you pick out an appropriate weight and color paper for the job. Show him your mock-up and let him know if you'll need more than one color ink or if you'll be using photographs.

Your production schedule (or lack of one) can kill your whole project before it gets off the ground and starts producing the results you're looking for. Decide *now* how often you will produce your newsletter over the next year. Then fill in the weeks between with all the responsibilities necessary to meet that schedule. You can publish your newsletter as often as monthly or as infrequently as semi-annually. Either bimonthly or quarterly is best. Name repetition is important to both public relations and advertising effectiveness. That schedule also gives you the opportunity to contact your clients in the off months with sales letters or other types of promotions.

As with advertising, fliers or brochures, your newsletter may not sell your listing. But don't get discouraged. You'll be building name and image recognition in your community and among your clients. And that is what sells houses.

8.
Get More out of Your Media with Public Relations

No advertiser ever has a big enough budget to place ads in every media. So in order to extend their advertising efforts, most businesses use public relations.

PR includes many different activities that work together to increase your identity in your market and improve public opinion about you. Your PR efforts might include joining or communicating with community organizations or governmental, business and political groups, or sponsoring charity and special events.

However, every PR program utilizes the media, whether or not it includes any other PR activities. Press releases, publicity releases and news or feature stories are the quickest, least expensive way to communicate with the general public or a particular market (through special-interest publications).

One reason is that publicity releases build credibility with an audience, since they are printed as part of the editorial section of the newspaper rather than as part of advertising. Your message carries more weight because the reader perceives it as coming from the newspaper rather than from you, the advertiser.

If you haven't made the most of press relations in the past, now's the time to start. This is true whether you're an independent real estate agent located in a one-newspaper town or if you're part of a national company that's spreading the word about its services from coast to coast.

If you fall down on your public relations, you're not doing all you can to get your name in front of potential clients.

Following are several ways to incorporate media opportunities into your public relations program.

The Press Release

One of the main communication tools used in public relations is the press release. This is an article that you submit to the newspaper with hopes that it will appear in print exactly the way you submitted it. This seldom happens, however, because the newspaper has the right to edit the release, shorten it or not use it at all.

Obviously, this is much different than advertising because an advertiser pays for his space and a press release is printed at no charge.

Furthermore, the ad runs exactly as it is submitted, provided it meets the paper's policy for good taste, etc.

Following is a sample press release that will give you an idea of the format most preferred by editors. Some ideas on the types of news and information you can use in a press release follow the sample.

```
XYZ Realty Group
1000 Forrest Drive
Real Estate, CA 92001

For: Immediate Release
Contact: Linda Lipman
213/424-8100
```

XYZ Realty Group Appointed Exclusive Sales Agents for Westchester's First Luxury Townhome Project

```
    Sales have begun on an $18
million townhome project in
Westchester, according to
Roger Gold of XYZ Realty
Group, exclusive sales agents
for the luxury project.
Morningside townhomes will
feature two or three bed-
rooms, vaulted ceilings,
fireplaces and panoramic
```

Sample Press Release

161

ocean views.

"We're receiving inquiries from across the county for these townhomes," Gold said. "One reason we believe the project will sell out quickly is that this is the first luxury townhome project in Westchester. Most homes in this area are more expensive single-family houses."

Prices for the homes range from $100,000 to $130,000 and below market rate financing is available to qualified buyers. The project developer is Wendell Industries and the architect is L.M. West, who has designed homes for upscale buyers for more than 30 years.

"In keeping with the amenities most in demand by today's townhome buyers, the project will feature a junior olympic size swimming pool and four tennis courts for residents' use. We've also been receiving favorable com- ments on the vast open space surrounding the homes," Gold added.

Models are open from 9

```
a.m. to 5 p.m. every day. To
visit the townhomes, take I-5
north to El Toro, turn east
to Morningside Drive and turn
left to the parking area.
    XYZ Realty Group also is
marketing the Shores, a
single-family residential
development in Eastlake and
Huntington Ridge, a condomin-
ium complex in Long Beach.

            -end-
```

Here are some tips for composing a professional press release:

1. The press release should be typed double-spaced on company letterhead with a contact person and phone number listed so the reporter can follow up on the release if necessary.

2. All releases should have a headline. Although the newspaper will probably change the headline, it instantly gives the editor the sense of the story. Keep in mind the five W's and H of reporting: who, what, where, when, why and how. Answer those questions in your article and you'll have a

complete story.

4. Write in newspaper style using quotations interspersed with summations. For a basic writing style, use a paragraph of quotes followed by a paragraph of facts. Keep your important information up front. If the editor is going to cut, it will most likely be from the bottom.

5. A good length for a press release is one to three pages. If your press release runs more than one page, type "more" at the end of each page and "end" at the bottom of the last page. Again, this is newspaper style and lets the editor know that more pages follow. Number each page.

Company News

If you're going to try to expand your advertising by using public relations, you'll probably want to stress your company's achievements to let your market know that you've been selling a lot of homes this year. That's a great idea! But do you think that your newspaper will write an article on how many homes you've sold? Chances are they won't see much news value in that story.

Furthermore, newspapers are usually so busy covering the news of the day — city council meetings, need for more schools, and the like — that they usually don't have enough reporters to cover publicity news from local companies.

Armed with this knowledge, you should be able to get more company coverage by doing two things: 1) Thinking like an editor by finding out the news angle to your story. 2) Supplying the information yourself (in a professionally done press release) rather than waiting for a reporter to come to you. Implement just those two concepts and you'll increase coverage of your company (or yourself) in the media.

Since the press release will appear as part of the editorial section of the paper, it must sound like an article, not an ad. A lot of what you want to advertise isn't appropriate for a press release at all. Trying to write a release on homes you have for sale usually won't work. You'll have to keep that type of news in your ads. But if you start thinking like an editor, you'll be able to squeeze some news stories out of your company business.

Following is a list of ideas of company stories that can be written as press releases. You can of course adapt these to your own needs and company.

1. New sales associate

2. New property management department, relocation department, etc.

3. Sales awards announced

4. Quarterly sales report announcing sales figures

5. Company charity event or sponsorship

6. Unusual home for sale

7. Opening of new office

8. New affiliation with national real estate network

9. American Home Week special events

10. Attendance at national conventions

11. New computer system

12. One-year (or ten-year or whatever) anniversary

13. Special events, such as First-Time Buyers Night

Note that most of these ideas are in some way related to "news": that which is new or unusual. However, you may not be able to use any of these ideas in your office if you keep running your organization the way it always has been run.

A better approach is to start thinking of

public relations opportunities and start *creating* them. If you don't have sales awards, maybe now is the time to start this program. If you don't calculate your quarterly sales (or the sales in your community), you could start this as well.

You also could start a quarterly forecast or become a sponsor of a charitable event or organization. If you attend a state or national real estate convention, issue a release when you return announcing news events from the convention, such as new mortgage programs or comparing local sales figures to national ones.

When your business news slows down, maybe it's time to hold a First-Time Home Buyers Seminar and issue news releases publicizing the event. These are some of the ways you can start creating your own news events and publicizing them.

National Events

Most likely, your newspaper will not publicize every company event you're involved with on a weekly basis. Another segment of your public relations campaign should focus on positioning your company as the local expert on national real estate news.

For example, after the Tax Reform Act of 1986 passed, the public became confused over the many changes in the massive tax overhaul, particularly changes affecting real estate. Here was an opportunity for a real estate broker or sales associate to offer his local audience and his potential clients the information on the new tax law. Since the changes were so complicated, this one "story" offered the opportunity to issue at least half a dozen news releases and half a dozen different stories that credit your name and company with the information or commentary. Here are some of the stories that could have been developed:

1. Changes affecting the ability to deduct points in the year paid in conjunction with refinancing a principal residence. Limitation restricting the amount of mortgage interest that can be deducted in a refinanced home to the cost of the home plus improvements, in most cases.

2. Elimination of capital gains treatment on profit from sale of investment real estate.

3. Elimination of mortgage interest deduction on more than two personal residences.

4. Changes affecting depreciation rates on investment real estate.

5. Reassurance that mortgage interest up to one million dollars and real estate taxes remain fully deductible on principal residence.

6. Limitations on deductions for passive losses from real estate investment.

Obviously, some of these issues are complex and you must be accurate in any information you submit to the media. But, this tax information was readily available to any real estate professional who wanted to spend a little time requesting a tax reform pamphlet from one of the "Big Eight" accounting firms, who were interested in promoting their own public relations.

However, the best way to handle national news stories is to feature a local angle. Most newspapers receive many more national press releases than they can use. But, if a local expert is featured or the national issue is brought down to the local level, papers and their readers become more interested.

In the tax story for example, the news release could discuss how tax reform will affect local home buyers or real estate investors — if the market will improve, where the local opportunities are for buyers now, or if more or less building will result in your hometown, for instance.

Features

The third part of your press release campaign should include entertaining or interesting timeless features. Most real estate sections are loaded with these, so obviously editors are receptive. Features also help you continue to get your name out to the real estate editors and your public throughout the year, not just when you have news or there is a big national story like tax reform.

As a real estate professional, you may offer advice or comment on a variety of issues, not just buying and selling homes. Your realm of expertise includes home building, financing, taxes, even interior decorating. Again, be sure that any information you release is accurate. Here are some feature ideas:

1. How to get your house ready for sale

2. The increasing number of home buyers who hire home inspectors

3. New financing programs particularly suited to first-time buyers

4. The value of a view in buying a home

5. The types of homes most appealing to senior citizens

6. New trends in interior decorating most in demand by home buyers

7. What trade-up buyers look for most in homes

8. The local real estate outlook for the rest of the year

9. Do condominiums make good first-time real estate investments?

10. Getting ready for closing: what is title insurance, escrow and the mound of paperwork that accompanies a real estate transaction?

You will be able to start your own idea file just from trends you see around you — a jump in the number of condominiums being sold, sudden demand for assumable loans or new community parks adding value to homes in the area. As you can see, all these stories have a timeless element in common.

Editors like these types of releases because they can be dropped in anytime the newspaper has room. They don't have to run on a certain day before they lose their relevance. You'll like that idea too, because you'll have more of a chance of your release being used since the editor isn't locked into only one day or week.

At first you might wonder how these stories are going to help you sell more homes. But remember that your major goal in public relations is getting people to *know* your name, think favorably of you, *remember* you and *think of* you first when they decide to buy or sell real estate.

Press releases that offer insights into real estate are read and remembered. They add to

171

your credibility as a knowledgeable, community-minded salesperson or broker — and that's the image you are building through your advertising. Combined with your total marketing efforts, newspaper articles will encourage people to call you first — before someone they haven't seen in the news.

Furthermore, your competition may start becoming a little intimidated. They'll pick up the newspaper, see your release and think, "How did he or she get in the paper again?" Soon, you may even find sales associates from other companies thinking the same thing and being envious of your firm.

Another benefit is that press coverage tends to build from each article. Did you ever notice that when you see a story in one newspaper, another paper covers the same topic and interviews the same sources shortly afterward?

The media tend to steal from each other. So if you get your story in one paper, chances are good that another paper will remember it and call you in the future when it is covering a real estate story or the other paper will print a similar story right away.

Press Relations

One of your goals in issuing releases and establishing yourself as the real estate expert in your community is to get the media to start regarding you the same way. You want them to think that anytime they're writing an article on real estate, they should call you to get your input, opinion or comment. You want them to think that if they don't call you, they don't have a complete story.

But writers and editors may not always think of you first. You must be on top of the situation. You wouldn't rely on someone who's visited your open house to call you the following day, would you? You would call them the following day to see if the property interested them. The same approach works with the media.

First, you need to learn the names of the writers and editors covering real estate. Next, call them and try to set up a meeting to discuss the types of real estate information and statistics you have available to share with them. Finally, start supplying them with the information they need along with a media kit on your company.

The media kit should have a two-page background article on your company, a one-page reference sheet on your company (listing the officers, principal business, branches, major sales of the year and so forth, in outline form), and any past articles that have appeared in the papers mentioning your company. You can also include a 5 x 7 inch or 8 x 10 inch black-and-white professional photo of yourself.

You should be in regular contact with real estate reporters and editors to find out what stories the newspapers are planning to cover on their own. Often, weekly papers or sections plan their features a month in advance and newspaper editors are usually very willing to share some of their topics with you because they're looking for sources for the articles. By finding out what they're planning on covering you know what type of information to supply. That increases your chances of being interviewed and mentioned in the story.

For example, a friendly meeting with your local editor could reveal that upcoming stories include:

1. Unusual occupations real estate salespeople have had before they turned to real estate.

2. A story on the traditional dilemma of buying a house first or selling your current home before you buy.

3. The types of home improvements that have the biggest payoff when it comes to resale.

By knowing these topics as they are developing, you can offer information and be part of the story. You may even be able to avoid picking up the paper, seeing your competitor's name in the article and saying, "Why wasn't I included?"

You can call or write editors with your side of the story. If a reporter calls you looking for information or quotes, be prepared to return calls quickly. Often reporters are working on deadlines and the sources who call them back first are the ones mentioned in the story, even if they aren't the largest real estate companies in the area.

Finally, while your press releases may not be printed at all, the editor will still read them and file your name away as a good source for real estate stories. Releases may even serve as the starting points for bigger stories later on. An article you submit on the effect of interest rates on real estate may lead to an article including your information as well as quotes from mortgage bankers. While you would not be the only source featured in this news story, you would still be the primary real estate source. That's good PR!

Pitch Letters and Tip Sheets

Newspapers are always looking for stories, but some never print press releases. They like to cover their own stories. Your press releases will still be helpful here, since the newspapers may save them and call you later to add more quotes to their story. Your goal, though, in working with many of these papers is to suggest stories that promote real estate investment and home ownership. Some editors, if left on their own, never see the positive side of the real estate industry. You don't want to leave the story ideas entirely up to them.

Some PR observers have said that about ninety percent of what we read in the paper is legitimate news. The other ten percent is made up of stories that have been planted by PR professionals. You want to get in on as much of that ten percent of editorial space as you can.

The best and most successful freelance writers don't wait for a publication to call them with a story idea — they supply their own. You can supply story ideas and accomplish your own PR goals at the same time. Besides supplying press releases, there are basically two ways to initiate story ideas with the media.

The first is the *query* or *pitch letter*. This is written as a personal letter to the editor or reporter trying to spark his interest in covering a story on his own, and of course, offering your help. Even though you may be tempted to use a more informal writing style in your letter, be sure it is professional in every way.

If you need to include statistics, make them accurate and convincing. Have your story well thought out and your angle very clearly defined before you write the letter.

Again, you should also try to make the story sound so appealing that he'd look like a fool if he didn't cover it and found it in his competing newspaper first. Following is a brief example:

```
Dear Real Estate Editor
(Use the real name):

    First-time home buyers are
virtually locked out of the
dream of home ownership in
Southern California because
of high mortgage interest
```

rates and high home prices. But now a new first-time buyer home loan plan is available through the county department of housing. The plan allows purchasers to buy much more home than they could afford if faced with today's interest rates. There are income and property restrictions, but a substantial number of the homes in (name of your town) qualify for the financing. This loan program is available only through the rest of this year. Because of all the government cutbacks, we may never see this type of financing again.

Several buyers I have worked with recently were unaware of the program. There is a need to inform your readers of the availability of funds and the qualifying procedures.

I have complete information on the program, am prepared to discuss how it will affect the local market (both buyers and sellers), and can

```
put you in touch with recent
clients who couldn't have
bought their homes without
the financing.

    I am offering this story
to only the (name of news-
paper) at this time. Please
let me know if you would like
to pursue the article. Thank
you for your prompt atten-
tion.

Sincerely,



Your name
```

In the last paragraph of the letter, the writer has offered the story as an "exclusive" to the paper. You can also do this with your press releases. Most newspapers like being offered a story first and the practice encourages them to cover the story. If the paper doesn't respond to your letter, you can follow up with a phone call. If the editor says he isn't interested in the story, you then can offer it to another publication.

The second way to direct news coverage is to provide quarterly or bimonthly *tip sheets* to the media. These can be written as query letters or you can design them as newsletters.

The difference between the pitch letter and

the tip sheet is that in the tip sheet, you offer several stories (about four or more), summarizing each idea in a paragraph or so.

The editor then can review several ideas at one time, choose what he feels is appropriate and follow up on those ideas only. Your chances are greater that he'll follow up on something you offer him in a tip sheet because you're offering more choices than in the single pitch letter.

A final way to get articles in the paper is to write them yourself. You have several choices here. The most obvious is to write an article under your own "byline" and submit it to the editor, a special interest publication or use it in your ad format. You wouldn't use any quotes in this article, since you would be the expert quoted throughout. Several ideas for article topics under your byline follow:

Write Your Own Column

- What to Look for in Buying Foreclosures

- Qualifying Procedures for FHA-Insured Financing

- What You Can Do to Be Sure Your House Purchase Closes on Time

Another common article is the question and answer column where you are the real estate expert answering all the questions. Again, you can write your own or look into several services that supply real estate columns of this nature. You simply write in your byline and submit the column to the paper.

However, before you order columns from a service for your own publicity, contact your newspaper first and see if it's interested in publishing such a column on a regular basis. Otherwise, you'll have to use the column as an ad and pay for the space.

These columns could appear as articles only, or you could invite readers to send you their questions. If you have the time, the second alternative could be quite attractive since it may provide you with actual names for leads.

Other PR Tools

Another way to get your byline in the paper is to write a letter to the editor. These are printed in the paper's "Letter to the Editor" section. You probably won't have much success if you submit letters every week talking about how many homes you sold last week. But if you use the letter to the editor to comment intelligently on local real estate issues, it's more likely to be printed. Keep it in mind if you need it.

You may see press conferences on the news every night and this tool is available to you as well. But use it very sparingly, if at all. If you call even one press conference haphazardly without releasing some astonishing news, you won't find the media coming to you again.

This type of unprofessionalism tends to

stick in the editors' minds. On the other hand, if all of your press releases, pitch letters, tip sheets and bylined articles are done well, you will get results. Knowledgeable, reliable and articulate sources are extremely valuable to the media. If you fall into that category, you'll be called often.

Some advertisers test a publication with a press release before they buy advertising in it. If you're considering advertising in a publication, but are not sure if the newspaper will pull for you, try submitting a press release.

PR as an Advertising Test

After it appears, see if you get any response, any comments from your salespeople or clients. You may be surprised to find out that a newspaper you were never considering seems to be the one read by your public. Your next step is to continue advertising regularly in that publication.

Unlike advertising, press coverage cannot be guaranteed even if you hire a PR professional. There's a fairly common belief among advertisers that if they advertise regularly, they're guaranteed to have their press releases printed and their officers interviewed for news stories. They may also believe that if they don't advertise at all, they won't be able to get anything into the newspaper. However, this is not standard policy at most newspapers. The editorial and advertising staffs are usually completely sepa-

No Guarantee

181

rate departments. In fact, it's best not to even mention to a newspaper editor that you're an advertiser. Most editors read their own papers and know their advertisers anyway. Reminding them that you're an advertiser injects an altogether unprofessional tone into your press relations.

If you ask ahead of time what types of articles the editor is looking for, you'll have a better chance of getting coverage for your press releases. If the editor hates tax articles, know it and avoid them. On the other hand, he may tell you that they're looking for some solid information on the tax advantages of home ownership. Writing an article on this topic, then, becomes a sure win.

Providing professional materials is one of the most important keys to getting coverage. But if it's a big news day with many more important stories than usual, newspapers find they need fewer "filler" stories and yours might fall into that category. Your story is also competing with every other release and story that comes into the newspaper office, so a different story might win that day.

If you want a guarantee, review the following amusing, but accurate commentary written by Barry Corday Fain, editor of *Southern California Land Magazine*, in an article in that publication.

**Five Ways to Guarantee Your
News Release is Thrown Out**

1. Have no idea what the publication
   even looks like, what it covers, the
   type of stories it prints and the
   manner in which they're written.
   Just mail out a story that interests you and hope the editor will
   run it!

2. Pay no attention to the publication's
   deadline. If you have an event
   taking place tomorrow, mail the
   release today!

3. Don't double-space and typewrite
   neatly on one side of a sheet of
   paper. Use a desk-top computer
   to create a mess that looks like
   Patton's Third Army just blasted
   its way across your hard-to-read
   paper. Then Xerox it and mail!

4. Use all capital letters, don't indent
   paragraphs, spell like a third-
   grader who's hiding from the
   truant officer and use slang from
   the wrong side of the tracks. It's
   so much better than good English!

5. Call the editor in a week and ask if he received your news release. He receives only scores every day, and the most important event in his life is keeping track of your news release!

9.
Choosing a PR or Advertising Agency

From time to time, you may want to work with an outside public relations or advertising agency. Or if the size of your brokerage or marketing budget requires it, you may need to keep an agency on retainer year-round.

There are several advantages to working with an agency. First, while their fees are not cheap, they are less expensive than retaining such talent as part of your full-time payroll.

A second benefit is that you are getting an outsider to look at your firm and to help you communicate with your audience. If you handle your own PR and advertising, there's a possibility that you'll end up talking to yourself and not those outside of your company.

Finally, you will gain by having your time freed for handling your daily real estate responsibilities, while the experts create your communications. Your goal is to have professional looking and sounding materials. If you're totally involved in marketing real estate and obtaining new clients, you may not have time to develop and write effective ads and PR. Recognize this and call in the pros. Following are the services you can expect from agencies and how you can expect them to work with you.

How an Agency Works

All agencies have a similar structure, whether they're organized as a one-person consulting firm based out of the individual's home or as companies with hundreds of employees and dozens of branch offices. Some agencies offer both public relations and advertising while others specialize in one or the other.

Whether it's for advertising or PR, when dealing with a large agency, clients usually deal directly with an account executive (AE). That means if you don't like the cartoon sketch that is proposed for your ad, you don't call the agency's art department, you tell your AE instead.

To make the most of the services of your AE, inform him of everything about your company. He also should be informing you about the media, your market and even real estate trends in your area. In larger agencies, the AE reports to an account supervisor. Be sure you have a good rapport with your AE. If not, ask for a new one.

After completing some market research on

the points to advertise, problems to be confronted, your current market and the market you hope to attract, your agency will start creating ads and deciding where to place them for you.

As a follow-up to the advertising design and placements, the agency also can keep track of your ads, making sure that they have run when and where they were supposed to and that you have been billed properly. For PR services, the agency should conduct similar marketing research before planning the program and selecting the media.

Agencies use a variety of billing procedures. Some work on the basis of the fifteen percent commission they receive from the media on your ad placements plus an hourly rate for agency services and a mark-up on outside vendors (photographers, designers, etc.) Others charge a monthly retainer in addition to the cost of any services.

In public relations, a monthly retainer that covers a specified number of hours (or less) is common. Be sure the agency clearly understands your budget requirements before you get started. In both PR and advertising, budgets can range from several hundred dollars a month to millions, depending on the media used and the sophistication you desire.

If you take your account to an agency that offers everything from television and radio production to casting directors and photographers, you'll probably be paying for that agency's

187

higher overhead and for services that you don't even need or use.

Don't be overly concerned if your budget is small; you can still make it work. You just have to be more careful about not wasting money. One way is to pay for only what you need. If you're looking for a series of well-designed institutional print ads that you can use for years, you may be able to use a free-lance copywriter and graphic designer for the creative services.

You could even handle your media buying yourself through your own internal agency to take advantage of the fifteen percent commission. Or you could use a media buying service, pay it a small percentage on the ads placed and take advantage of the fifteen percent commission offered by the media to the service.

When buying public relations services, see if you can pay for each article, rather than a retainer fee. A PR agency usually charges for hours rather than placements. You may be lucky one month and get three articles in the paper and then you may not see anything in print for several months. However, if you were paying a retainer, you would still be paying the same fee for each of those months, no matter how many articles were placed.

On the other hand, if you pay for each placed article, the agency then would charge you one fee for writing the article and another placement fee when the article appears somewhere. Although this sounds like you would be paying double, it could actually be less costly than paying a high monthly retainer fee for articles that rarely appear in print.

Where do you find the agency miracle workers? Here are a few tips on what to look for when choosing an agency.

What to Look For

1. Every agency will show you samples, but the truth is that you'll be seeing the agency's best work, not its daily progress on your account.

   Besides looking for work that you like, look for people you like. As a client, you will need to critique your agency's work and the agency in turn, will need to tell you what you've been doing wrong. That type of communication must be built on a strong rapport or your relationship will always be under some stress.

   Even though you may have spent time looking for the right personality mix, you may find that after you sign an agreement the people you were planning on working with have left the agency.

   This isn't uncommon in advertising or PR where turnover is fairly high. Be prepared to go

189

through the process again and make sure that anyone taking over your account has the knowledge and experience to work for your company as well as the personality that will mesh with your own style. If not, insist that your contract be terminated.

2. Find an agency that understands the real estate industry and believes in your company. You don't want to have to start from scratch telling your agency all about real estate and the factors that go into a home buying or selling decision.

On the other hand, if you are steered to an agency that handles many other real estate accounts, you may not be the brokerage that comes first in their minds when they recommend someone to the media for interviews. When they have a great idea for an ad, it may go to your competitor rather than to you.

Your agency should believe that you are responsible, competent and highly professional in real estate. If they don't, they should decline your account.

If the agency handles other real estate clients, establish first if

there are any conflicts of interest
before you get started. Be sure
you understand what the
agency's policy is in case a competing company approaches them
as a client in the future.

3. Trust is important. You are hiring
professionals; treat them as such.
You don't have to agree with everything your account executive
tells you, but if he comes up with
sound reasons for his ideas, trust
him as being the professional
you've hired and let him do his job
without interfering.

You also want to work with
people you can trust about money
matters — who will get your
printing, art and design and so
forth done at reasonable rates
and bill you appropriately. If
you're constantly questioning
bills, you might as well get the
work done yourself.

4. Look for experience and reputation.
Ask your ad salespeople at the
media you normally advertise in
for recommendations. If the
agency deals with the local media, the salespeople should know
which ad agencies do the best,

most professional work. Ask the real estate editors at the local papers which public relations agencies suggest the freshest story ideas, presented in the most usable style.

5. Big agencies can be impressive in appearance and quality of presentation. But if you're a small account, you probably won't get the attention that you need to achieve your goals.

    The best advice here is to select an agency large enough to cover all the services you are looking for, but small enough so that you will be a major account. Your agency size should approximately match your brokerage size. The same goes for selecting a legal or accounting firm. Smaller professional consulting firms work best with smaller businesses. Larger firms usually go after larger accounts.

6. *Creative* is a buzzword in advertising. Some agencies won't release anything that doesn't draw attention to the ad itself and then to the agency that produced it. But that type of creativity doesn't always

draw in customers for clients. If you think the agency's style is creative, that's fine. But check with their clients to see if the ads helped improve business.

7. Look for variety. Agencies are only as good as the creative people who work in them. Most people have a certain style that they've developed and are comfortable using, so much of the work coming out of the agency may look similar.

    However, make sure that the agency you choose doesn't always use the same assembly line style. You want the agency to adapt to your needs; you don't want to have to adapt to the needs of the agency because it only has one advertising style.

8. Don't be sold by the presentation alone. Getting clients is half the battle for agencies but keeping them is the other half. Some agencies put all their efforts into attracting new business and their presentations show it: fancy notebooks, market research, even slide shows.

    But what's going to keep your account going past the initial presentation? Ask to see the last three ads they completed — not the best three ads they've done. Also ask the agency how many of its clients have stayed with them for more than one year.

Advertising is one of the most volatile industries in the country. It's very important to consider an agency's stability when you are deciding whether or not to give it your account.

9. Look for excitement and enthusiasm. Your agency should think that creating ads for your account is a challenging opportunity that they will enjoy. They should be proud of their work and proud to work with you. Look for this attitude.

10. Plan on staying somewhat involved. Ask the agency how much input you will be required to give. Obviously, you shouldn't have to write ads, but you will need to communicate your goals to the agency.

On the public relations side, your story ideas should always be welcome. But the agency should be able to provide enough of its own ideas (and of course, the manpower to put the ideas into action), to continually generate stories about your company and real estate.

You should be in the position of just approving the story ideas and then approving the completed articles before they are submitted to the press. Be wary of a company that will sit back and wait for you to suggest all the stories.

On the other hand, your agency may be suggesting stories to the media rather than writing them. If the media are interested in covering the story, you should expect to be available for the interview. Very few reporters will be satisfied interviewing your PR counsel or one of your subordinates. If you insist on not being quoted, chances are the reporter will interview another real estate professional who is available for direct quotes and probably not call you again.

Appoint someone who will be the liaison between your company and the agency and be responsible for quick approvals. Editing by committee never seems to work. The changes one person wants to make, another person disagrees with. By the time an entire committee approves a press release and returns it to the agency, for dissemination, the news may be too old to be of interest.

Deciding When It's Time for a Change

The beginning of your relationship with an agency is the time to get to know each other. Give your agency at least several months before you make any harsh judgments. Then compare your media exposure with that of your competitors' and see if your advertising has a more professional look and is meeting your goals.

Further down the line, meet more formally with your AE and discuss any problems and progress. This will let the agency know that they are going in the right direction or that if they don't change, you'll make a change.

If your PR or advertising agency is out of ideas, it's time to look for a new firm. This does happen, so watch out for it. Some agencies just lose their ability to produce new concepts that capture attention for their clients after working with them for awhile. If this happens, meet with the head of the agency and discuss the problem. You may be satisfied with a new AE instead of going to a new agency. This at least gives them the opportunity to get back on the right track before they become your "former" agency.

You can save a lot of money on the production end of your materials if you do it yourself. But if your materials are unprofessional, it could cost you dearly by wasting the money you paid on the space. Don't make the mistake of buying a lot of time and space without a lot of talent. Spend what you need to on production to get your advertising done right, even if it means cutting from your space budget.

Even if you don't hand over all of your advertising to an agency, try to reserve some of your annual advertising budget for professional production. That doesn't mean that you must sign an annual contract with an ad or PR agency. But it does mean you should use professional services when you need them.

For example, you should work with an artist on producing your logo. Is $1,000 a big expense for a logo? It is if it turns out to be useless. But if you're going to use the logo on your letterhead, ads, business cards, brochures and fliers for years to come, that cost can be amortized over years.

If you're talented as a writer and graphic artist, you're probably qualified to write ads. But that will take you away from your day-to-day real estate business. So any money you save by not hiring an outside professional will be lost on the business you're not taking care of.

If you're short on time and can build trust with an agency, that's definitely the way to go. The agency will handle your entire advertising program for you. But you can also establish your

Who Handles What

197

own relationships with free-lancers — photographers, artists, copywriters, media buying services, marketing consultants.

A good copywriter for your account may be retired from a big agency. A good PR practitioner may be retired or moonlighting from his newspaper job. If you go this route, you'll need to do some legwork to find writers, graphic designers, photographers, illustrators, typographers and such. Sometimes these professionals know each other, so ask for referrals. When you find a copywriter, ask him the name of a graphic designer and ask for estimates ahead of time from each.

Your materials won't come cheaply and your image won't become a household name overnight. However, think about your advertising investment as one that should pay dividends over time. When you must spend a great deal for a piece, think of other ways you can use it — as a flier, brochure or even a sign for your office. Try to get some designs that can be used over and over for years so they won't cost as much as those produced for a one-time use only.

Since classified advertising is the bulk of the real estate brokerage's advertising, it's better to let your office handle it, rather than the agency. You're not going to want to use an agency to decide which listings to advertise for you each week. But your agency could design a display layout that can be reused weekly by dropping in different listings. The agency will be concerned with developing your institutional program, rather than ads for each listing.

If the salespeople are writing the ads and the managers are checking them and deciding which ones to run each week, another function is still left: double-checking the wording before the ads go out and the bills after the ads run. These important functions should be handled by a highly qualified and detail minded individual in the office.

10.
Don't Keep Your Advertising a Secret

Record keeping is essential to maintaining your business organization and productivity. Information on how many listings you have, how many you had last year, how much your quarterly income is and how much you owe in taxes must be calculated regularly.

If you decide to keep these figures to yourself, that's fine. But when it comes to keeping track of your advertising, you must share the information with your broker (if you're a sales associate), the other salespeople in your office and, in order to make the most of your efforts, the seller. You also need to be prepared to handle any "up calls" from clients who see your ads.

This chapter will discuss some ways to help you meet these responsibilities.

Once you've taken a listing, you'd better be prepared to get calls — not only about your listing, but from the seller, himself. The seller will either call to find out when his house was advertised or will call as a result of seeing your ad on his property. A tracking system for classified ads is invaluable for handling these calls.

First, the Seller

One system uses a monthly master notebook. The first page is a list of properties and the calendar for the month. Down one side is the address of each listed property and the expiration date of the listing so you don't accidentally advertise the property after the listing has expired.

Across the top is a list of all the days of the month. Every time an ad is run on the property, an "X" is marked in the box under the day the ad ran. When the property sells, the listing is lined out. All new listings are added as they come in.

The rest of the notebook is organized with dividers for each property. Behind each divider are copies of all the ads that have run with the date and name of the newspaper stamped on each ad.

When the seller calls saying that he hasn't seen an ad on his property in weeks, the listing agent can open the notebook, look at the first page and say, "Yes, Mr. Seller, I can understand your concern. Let me check our schedule. Your home was advertised on the first, tenth and twentieth of this month. May I read the ads to you?"

Then, the agent can turn to the divider

201

section and read the ads and mention where they appeared. Because the system is very simple, any agent can handle these questions and anyone in the office can be responsible for the book. If you can respond that quickly to calls from your sellers, they will be impressed.

However, you may not want to wait for a call from the seller to let him know that you're advertising his home. One way of keeping in touch with sellers is to clip each ad as it appears and paste it to a postcard with your personal note. Some sellers will appreciate getting your notes in the mail — but not all. Some of them make more unfavorable comments and ask you why the ad wasn't longer, or bigger, or run more often. You'll have to see if the cards result in favorable comments from your sellers.

Use The Ads to Get The Listing

One way of getting the listing, writing the ads and keeping your seller informed at the same time is to prepare ads for the listing presentation before the agreement is signed with the seller.

One company uses a computerized system for writing classified ads. After the agent visits the home and makes some notes (fireplace, two stories, four bedrooms, one acre, etc.), he goes back to the office where he types the data into the system. The computer program organizes the data and creates a headline for several different ads. On the second listing appointment, the agent presents the ads and asks the seller, "Which ad should we start with?" With the seller's answer, "I like the one with the headline: Executive Estate," the agent has the listing.

Presenting the ads at the listing appointment helps you get a signed agreement, gets the ads written and shows the seller the classified ads you're planning to use.

Besides showing the seller ads for his own property at the listing presentation, you'll definitely want to show him ads you've run for other listings as well as other advertising, marketing and promotional materials. Order additional stats or ad slicks from the publications you've advertised in to show during listing presentations. If you've advertised in some prestigious magazines, don't keep it a secret. Remember, one of your main reasons for advertising is to satisfy the listing. Go ahead and show off your ads.

Be Prepared for Calls From Sellers

Some sellers will call your office asking about an advertised listing that is actually their house. They are checking to see how calls about their home are being handled. These are probably sellers who have told their listing agent how valuable the skylights are or how they've spent thirty years nurturing their grove of fruit trees.

If these features haven't been mentioned in the ad and aren't discussed when the seller calls, he could become a little emotional. Since you never know when and if a seller is going to check on you this way, be sure you are familiar with all the seller's "hot buttons" and communicate them to all callers.

Second, Salespeople and Brokers

Ads don't sell homes. When calls come in, they must be handled professionally to get results. Keeping salespeople informed of the ad schedule helps them to prepare for "up calls."

First of all, a sales associate isn't ready to handle calls until he's seen most of the office listings. After all, the office listings are the properties featured in the ads. Be sure all salespeople are kept routinely up-to-date on *all* office listings — not just on their own individual listings.

Salespeople must then be trained in effective telephone techniques for handling calls. While all salespeople want the name and phone number of the potential prospect, most callers resist giving this information to any salesperson. You must invest some time qualifying the buyer and learning his needs, before asking for his name and number. This is a more successful approach most of the time.

Following is a proposed script for handling "up calls" from ads. You can adapt this to the specific needs of the caller and use a switch sheet to set up appointments.

UP CALL SCRIPT

Caller: "I'm calling about your

ad for the four bedroom
home."

Agent: "Yes, can you tell me the
headline on that ad please?"

Caller: "It's the Family Delight. Where is that home
located?"

Agent: "It's in Willow Walk. Is
that an area you were interested in?"

Caller: "Well, not really."

Agent: "We have another four
bedroom home in Spring Grove.
Were you looking for a four
bedroom home?"

Caller: "Yes."

Agent: "And the price?"

Caller: "Well, actually, we
didn't want to go as high as
the advertised price."

Agent: "The Spring Grove four
bedroom is an outstanding
value. It doesn't have a
pool, but it has a fireplace

and air conditioning and light neutral colors. It's really in top condition and the price is $10,000 lower.

By the way, it's four blocks to the school. Do you have children?"

Caller: "Yes, I have two kids. Well, I'll call you later. I have some other homes to look into."

Agent: "To save you time and confusion, I'd be happy to look up any other advertised homes in the paper for you. I can get the information and call you back.

This is Linda Lipman. By the way, who am I talking to?"

Caller: "Mrs. Singer."

Agent: "Mrs. Singer, where can I reach you?"

Notice how the agent offers a little information in the responses to the caller's questions but then ends the response with a question to further qualify the buyer. Build some rapport with the caller before you ask for name and phone number and always ask if other ads have been circled. That gives you a reason to call back later.

A tracking book helps sales associates to keep track of all the "up calls" received for all listings advertised during the week. It should be available to each sales associate on the floor.

Keep a Tracking Book

Use the first page of the book to record all calls for the week. This page should be used to record the date and time the call came in, the property address, the source of the call (whether it be ad, yard sign or referral) and the result of the call. Sales associates should also routinely ask callers where they heard about the listing and record this information.

You'll want to keep track of the media, the day of the week the ad was run and the appeal used in the headline. That way you'll have a more useful report showing the best days to advertise, the newspapers pulling the highest response and the types of headlines that draw the most.

Copies of or actual listing ads clipped from the newspaper should also be kept in the tracking book. But that's not really going far enough in keeping salespeople informed. There should also be a listing sheet and a switch sheet for each ad.

The switch sheet is a list of all other office listings in the same price category (if there are any) as well as any listings in the Multiple

Listing Service that are either in that price range or a nearby area.

That way, when a prospect calls on an ad, the sales associate is not only prepared to discuss the advertised property in detail from the listing sheet and his own knowledge of the listing, but can also "switch" the caller to another listing if needed. This could turn a prospect call into a prospect sale.

Chances are that the ad alone won't sell the property. You may not even be able to schedule a showing for the advertised house, if the rest of the details on the property don't fit the caller's needs. Being prepared to discuss properties comparable to those being advertised is essential to making the most of "up calls."

The best way to do this is by having a switch sheet ready. This sheet allows you to quickly see the advertised listing along with other homes in the same price range. You can copy the following switch sheet and use it in your own tracking book.

SWITCH SHEET

Ad Headline _____

Price/Terms _____

Address _____

Bedrooms/Baths _____

Features _____

_____

Switch #1 Address _____

Price/Terms _____

Bedrooms/Baths _____
Features _____
_____

Switch #2 Address _____
Price/Terms _____
Bedrooms/Baths _____
Features _____
_____

Switch #3 Address _____
Price/Terms _____
Bedrooms/Baths _____
Features _____
_____

Ad Headline _____
Price/Terms _____
Address _____
Bedrooms/Baths _____
Features _____
_____

Switch #1 Address _____
Price/Terms _____
Bedrooms/Baths _____
Features _____
_____

Switch #2 Address _____
Price/Terms _____
Bedrooms/Baths _____
Features _____
_____

Switch #3 Address _____
Price/Terms _____
Bedrooms/Baths _____
Features _____

209

Keeping Brokers Informed

Brokers need to know how effective their advertising dollars are. Sales associates should give a report to management after each sale noting how that client was obtained. This will help the management determine which media are most effective in attracting qualified, income-producing prospects.

However, the best way to keep brokers informed about their own advertising effectiveness is through the log tracking system where all inquiries are recorded. But keeping just a record of the number of responses is only one part of judging results from your ads.

The next step is analysis. The broker is responsible for analyzing ads and sharing the information with the salespeople on a periodic basis. This analysis is an ongoing problem — or opportunity — that changes with market conditions. Because one newspaper is pulling the best this year doesn't mean it should never be changed in the future. Getting the right mix of the media, the copy, the property and the appeal is a continual process.

11.
Your Accountant Will Ask For It — The Advertising Budget

When you're putting together your business plan or your annual budget, you know you'll have fixed expenses for accounting fees, board fees, rent, utilities and insurance. These are all the costs of doing business as a broker. Sales associates also should budget for standard operating costs, such as membership in the Board of Realtors and car expenses.

But marketing isn't part of your fixed costs. It's the easiest item to relegate to the bottom of your expenses for the year, after you've bought the pens and pencils. For many real estate professionals, advertising is the first item to be cut when they're not meeting their budgets. While you may be tempted to just allocate money toward advertising when you have money, this is a mistake. Strict budgeting is necessary for advertising or the cost can quickly become overwhelming.

Most business people don't have any objection to spending money on advertising if they believe they'll make money from it. The problem is that they don't know which advertising dollars, if any, will be multiplied and then returned to them. Marketing isn't always easy to track. It may be difficult to see which advertising is bringing in the highest return. This chapter will discuss your advertising budget and help you evaluate the results of your ads.

Where's the Money Going to Come From?

There are many ways to set an advertising budget: by listing, by sales associate, by expected income, by gross sales and so on. But basically you can get advertising funds from three sources:

1) broker
2) sales associate
3) seller

The Broker

If you belong to a brokerage that is either owned by a national corporation or is part of a national franchise, you might be able to consider that a fourth source, even though you are ultimately paying for those ads.

The broker's advertising budget normally covers an institutional program to get the name of the company recognized in the local community and a budget to advertise the company's listings. Many brokers combine both messages in their ads. For example, if a block ad for listings is placed, one-fifth of the ad might be used to:

- offer a coupon for a free market analysis
- include photos of each sales associate
- use display type to announce: "We Guarantee You an Open House Every Week Your Home Is Listed With Us"

These elements are all institutional messages combined with the blocks of copy describing each home for sale in the ad. Even if you don't include an institutional message, your listing advertising works to say: "Other people have bought the idea that we can sell their home. Here are the other people and here are their homes. Your home could be here, too."

The Sales Associate

The sales associate can do the same type of advertising, combining listings and image building. Some companies offer salespeople a higher commission split but expect the associate to pay for more of the advertising if more advertising is wanted or needed.

In highly competitive areas, salespeople

routinely take out display ads for their listings and for their images (the office within the office concept). But this is very costly, especially for the beginning sales associate. A more economical alternative is to pool advertising resources with other sales associates in the office, to take out a bigger ad and offer more listings.

Since most sales associates who sell homes work as independent contractors, the amount of advertising they place and pay for varies widely. If a broker needs to reduce advertising in a certain publication that has been popular with the salespeople, he should first ask them if they would like to continue the advertising and split the cost. The salespeople may agree to it.

The Seller

The third source for advertising funds is the seller. In the typical transaction, however, the seller incurs no cost until the sale is closed. Therefore, the seller might be hesitant about spending money on marketing his property as well as paying the full commission on its sale.

But what if the seller wants extensive advertising? That's a big risk for the broker since very few ads result in the sale of the advertised listing. And if the property is undesirable, has a high price or has other drawbacks that make a quick sale unlikely, advertising may be the least of the factors that would bring a sale.

In a case like this, asking the seller to initially pay for some of the advertising may be appropriate, as well as acceptable to the seller. For instance, you could tell the seller that you will advertise his home twice a month.

If he would like it advertised more often, suggest that he pay for the extra ads up front. Once the house sells, you can reimburse him. That way, if his house sells during the listing, he hasn't actually paid for the advertising. But if his house remains unsold, you haven't paid for extra advertising that hasn't had any result.

On the other hand, if inventory is low, the house is priced right and the property is desirable, you may be able to sell the listing in two weeks. In this case, guaranteeing that you'll advertise it weekly may not be a risk at all, but a big benefit if the guarantee rewards you with a listing that sells quickly.

In cases of very expensive homes or unique properties, the seller often pays for extensive marketing materials such as brochures, direct-mail pieces or advertising in up-scale magazines directed at the affluent market.

If a property demands worldwide marketing, a film crew may be needed to prepare a video cassette for distribution.

Clearly, these are risky costs only suitable for unusual homes. Sellers should be expected to pay for them up front without being reimbursed by the sales associate, even if the property does sell.

How Much Should You Spend?

Before you decide how much to spend, think back to the reasons you advertise. Two of the main considerations here are what the competition is spending and what you can afford. But these two factors may pull your budget in opposite directions. Your competition may be spending thousands of dollars a month, but their listings, sales and sales force may be much bigger than yours enabling them to afford a bigger advertising budget.

While you may want to match or outdo your competition in advertising, realistically, you may not be able to afford to base your budget on what the competition is spending until your own sales and income increase.

Plan Spending Based on Income

For starters, keep in mind that you should allocate between five and fifteen percent of your expected gross income to advertising. (Most brokerages fall into this range.) That's after you've deducted commissions paid to sales associates. Chances are you won't be able to maintain or improve your business if you spend below the minimal five percent of income. However, if you're just opening your doors, plan on spending a higher percentage, especially in the initial months or it will take you longer to get established.

Sales associates, too, should plan an advertising budget based on their expected sales and income for the year. In fact, a top Canadian real estate sales associate (commissions over

$600,000 in 1986) attributes much of his success to the amount he spends on developing his business. "It's very important to invest in yourself," he advises.

If you base your budget on your expected income rather than on what the competition is spending, you know that you should be able to afford your advertising. This method will also force you to project your sales for the year, whether you're just starting out or can base the figure on what you've sold in the past.

When you're determining your projected income, you'll have to think about the coming market conditions. Will you be able to continue at the same pace as last year? Will you be able to increase sales? Do you want to increase sales? What will you have to do to increase those sales: more marketing, advertising, increase sales staff?

For example, if you're thinking that you can increase your income next year by two percent, then plan on increasing your advertising budget by at least two percent.

If you're going to plan a year in advance, you don't want to go through your annual advertising budget in one month. Once you decide on the dollar amount you will spend for the year, plan how that money will be used month-by-month. New brokerages or salespeople should consider doing a grand opening promotion or seasonal advertising. You should plan on spending more

Formulating Your Budget

in the spring and fall and less during the latter part of the year when business generally slows down.

Keep ten to twenty percent of your total budget flexible. That way you can take advantage of special editorial or advertising sections that become available, special deals or just an advertising alternative you hadn't thought about in the beginning of the year. Some magazines periodically have "remnant" or "distress" space left over from a big advertiser who didn't buy space in every geographic zone. This space is then sold at a discount to an advertiser who can use that zone.

One of the best ways to arrive at a monthly budget is by using the percentage of your expected monthly income. For example, if sixteen percent of your annual income will come in April, then sixteen percent of your advertising budget should be spent that month. Following is the monthly allocation of a $36,000 annual advertising budget:

Month	Percentage of Income	Ad Budget
January	6	$ 2,160
February	5	1,800
March	12	4,320
April	16	5,760
May	14	5,040
June	10	3,600
July	6	2,160
August	6	2,160

September	8	2,880
October	9	3,240
November	4	1,440
December	4	1,440

Using these figures as a guideline, review the rate cards from the various media in the area and allocate a portion of the monthly budget to each publication you have selected. Keep in mind volume discounts from the media so minimums are met.

After you determine monthly allocations, you can break down this figure for each publication on a weekly basis. With a calendar in front of you, plug in the days of the week you will advertise and the amount you will spend in each publication. That way when your ad rep comes calling, you can show him that you really do have a weekly ad budget established for his paper.

If your budget is too small to advertise every month in the media of your choice and if you can only afford a small ad once a month in an obscure publication, don't bother. Instead, try for brief, but intensive advertising campaigns several times a year. This is a more effective way of allocating a small budget than spreading it thinly throughout the year.

For example, if your budget is $1,000, spend $300 in January, $300 in April and the remainder in September. Don't think that you can change buying patterns drastically by advertising more in months that have traditionally been slow in real estate sales, such as November and December.

Advertise when you're going to hit the biggest market of ready, willing and able buyers. Have you ever noticed how thick newspapers and magazines are in November and December? Retailers know that these are the big holiday buying months when the buyers are out in full force. When business is quieter, in July and August for example, advertising drops off as well.

However, due to wide interest rate fluctuations in recent years, there are no longer hard and fast rules guaranteeing a winter slow season and a spring pickup in sales. If mortgage interest rates suddenly escalate in spring, your expected home buyers could disappear. On the other hand, if mortgages are offered at bargain rates in the winter, "fence-post sitters" may come out of the woodwork. Consequently, you should watch the economy and be prepared to start doing more marketing if you see that the business is out there.

After you've determined how much to spend annually, how much to spend monthly and where to spend it, you face one more decision. How much should you spend on property advertising versus image advertising? Many brokers allocate about twenty percent of their total budget to institutional advertising because they believe that their listing ads help their images, too. You can consider this ratio, but adapt it to your own needs and market.

If you don't feel that you can project a year in advance, at least plan three to six months in advance. Many newspapers will offer a discount if the advertiser's contract extends for that minimum time period. When you're two months into your contract, you'll probably be able to start planning for the next few months.

Writing the Budget

Salespeople should be aware of the broker's advertising budget and know if the office is over budget. One way of directly involving them is to allocate a budget for each sales associate based on a percentage of the total monthly budget.

In an article in the March, 1982 issue of *Real Estate Today*, Realtor John J. Henry of Lansing, Michigan describes a system of controlling ad costs that involves each sales associate in the office.

At the beginning of the month, management announces the monthly classified advertising budget and then calculates the number of listings each salesperson has and the total number of listings for the office. Each sales associate is then given a budget based on the percentage of the total listings he is carrying. Example:

April Classified Advertising Budget: **$4,608**
(80% of $5,760 total monthly budget)

Number of Office Listings: 100

Sales Associate	Listings	Percent of Budget	Budget
Smith	5	4,608x.05	$ 230
Jones	10	4,608x.10	$ 460
Alpine	20	4,608x.20	$ 921
Abrams	5	4,608x.05	$ 230
Gold	10	4,608x.10	$ 460
Foster	10	4,608x.10	$ 460
Beck	25	4,608x.25	$1,152
Lettner	10	4,608x.10	$ 460
Willard	5	4,608x.05	$ 230

This system has some pros and cons. One benefit is that the salesperson knows in the beginning of the month how much will be spent on advertising his listings. If he then wants to add to that company budget, he can. This way, the company isn't showing any preference any one listing or sales associate. This system also encourages salespeople to go out and get listings so they can have something to advertise.

If the listing agent is actually placing the ads himself, he can include his name in the ad. For this to work effectively, the office would use a client services coordinator (or secretary). When an "up call" comes into the office, the coordinator directs the call to the listing agent, who is the best resource on the advertised home.

Some offices claim that this system is far more efficient than having an ad call go to just anyone on the floor. As a listing tool, sales associates can tell their sellers that generally, calls will be handled by the listing agents themselves, not just anyone in the office. Consequently, the listing agent may be able to show the house more often.

This system eliminates much of the assigned floor time and gets salespeople out of the office so that they can be more productive. Salespeople should have paging devices, however, so they can be located quickly for their calls.

The salespeople would also be expected to write their own ads, with help from the broker or another more qualified individual. Listing agents should be responsible for writing at least a rough draft for a classified ad, since they are the most familiar with the property.

For example, the listing agent knows the seller's "hot buttons." He may believe that his wood deck should be mentioned in all ads. Sometimes, this type of understanding and compliance is crucial to having a smooth relationship with the seller. On the other hand, salespeople shouldn't be left on their own in the ad writing department. The broker or another designated, talented and organized individual should edit the ads.

Now for some disadvantages of the system: One problem with giving the salesperson an ad budget is that the next logical step is for him to place his own ads. This practice could break all the momentum that an office is trying to establish. For example, if your office is trying to advertise a block or even a full page of listings, you would still want only one person deciding where to place the ad.

Signing contracts with newspapers to take advantage of discounts also would be difficult if salespeople were advertising wherever and whenever they chose.

Another consideration is that you may not want to advertise every property with the same frequency. If a listing is several months old, is overpriced or needs some other adjustment for a likely sale, a change may be in order before more advertising dollars are spent on the listing. Another listing may be better suited for heavier advertising. If the phone rings every time a particular ad runs, you would probably want to advertise this listing much more often.

The final thought on the system is the handling of new listings during the month. Would there be enough budget left to advertise them?

Controlling the Budget

Budgets usually look great on paper, but as market conditions change, cost cutting or other changes may be needed. In that case, your goal should be to cut costs without sacrificing quality. Here are some suggestions:

Don't Advertise Similar Properties Simultaneously

Don't advertise two similar properties in the classified section at the same time. If handled properly, one ad could serve to initiate inquiries for both homes. Also, check to see if you can run a smaller ad at a lower price. Become efficient at cutting excess words to save lineage charges.

Make Your Display Ads Smaller
Try reducing the size of your display ads slightly. You may be able to generate the same response at a lower cost per ad.

Try Co-op Ads
Try co-op ads with other retailers in your shopping center or join forces with other companies serving the real estate industry, such as title insurance, homeowner's insurance or mortgage lending. You may be able to buy a larger space than you could on your own, at a lower cost.

Eliminate Unproductive Advertising
Cut back on any advertising that isn't paying its way. High school theater programs may be good community relations but poor response generators.

Beware of Volume Discounts
Media discounts are great, but before you sign a long-term contract guaranteeing a certain number of inches, find out what the consequences will be if you can't meet the minimum. You may need to cut back later in the year if you're over budget. Most media will send you a final bill at the end of the year charging you the higher rate if you haven't met your minimum.

Consider an In-House Agency
If you regularly advertise in the major metropolitan daily newspapers and magazines, consider establishing an in-house ad agency. Many

publications offer agencies a commission, normally fifteen percent of the space cost. If you're advertising with any volume, you could be saving fifteen percent of your advertising space charges by placing your advertising through your in-house agency.

If you already use an ad agency, ask if the company will credit your account for the fifteen percent commission it receives on your business. If that's not acceptable, see if it will research media for you and handle other advertising services at no charge in exchange for the fifteen percent commission.

Evaluating Your Advertising Effectiveness

You can't place enough ads that directly boost listings and sales. But an ad that hasn't accomplished its objective should be eliminated as quickly as possible. The question is how can you measure the results from your advertising program? You must realize that the many objectives in real estate advertising aren't always immediately obvious. Measuring how effectively your advertising has met all of your goals isn't easy.

Most advertising is profit-motivated. After all, if you haven't made money this year, you haven't convinced enough people to buy real estate from you. Furthermore, if you have increased your advertising budget this year, you expect to see your income increase, too.

At first, you may think that if your listing hasn't sold, your ad was wasted. But on second thought, your objective may be just to get your phone to ring. After a little more consideration, you may be happy if your ad has been noticed by a client or even if your sales associate comments that he feels good about the company's advertising.

These are all ways to judge ad effectiveness. But they're not the only ways.

One real estate office placed a two-page ad in the local Yellow Pages directory. Management and the sales associates pooled their resources to pay for the large ad. The primary objective was not to sell listings or even to make the phone ring. They wanted to feel that they were the biggest company in town. They wanted their competition to feel intimidated when they opened the Yellow Pages to check on their own ads. They knew that their two-page spread would be the largest of the ads placed by real estate companies. This office had satisfied its objective with that ad.

Much of your advertising will need time to build — the same way it's important to continue farming a neighborhood over time. Even though you may not see an immediate increase in your net income, if people keep noticing your name connected with a positive message, they will eventually try your office.

Obviously, factors other than advertising contribute to the profitability of a company or salesperson. If you're not prepared to handle the call you'll lose the potential client, even though he noticed your ad. If your rent or other costs are too high, you'll have a more difficult time making a bigger profit until you get those costs in line. If interest rates are high, your goals for the year may not be met but that would be generally true throughout the industry. So not showing a big enough profit immediately doesn't necessarily mean that your advertising was wasted.

Is selling the advertised listing a good indicator of the ad's effectiveness? The seller will certainly think so, and that's the presumed purpose of the ad. But if you've been in real estate any length of time at all, you know that selling a listing from an ad is rare.

More realistically, most salespeople would say that you've accomplished something if you receive calls from the ad. And if you get an "up call" and ultimately sell that caller another property better suited to him, the ad was very effective. It brought you a client, sale and income that you wouldn't have had without the ad. Even if you just get calls from the ad, without sales, that ad is doing its job of communicating desirable benefits about the house and about working with you.

Do People Notice Your Ads?

Judging the effectiveness of a strictly institutional message is more difficult. One way is to hire a market research team or commission some sophisticated studies to evaluate the ad's effectiveness. Another way is to periodically conduct some informal telephone surveys. Following are some points to cover in the survey:

1. Have people in your market area seen your ads?

2. Had they heard about your services before you started placing the ads?

3. Do they remember anything you said in the ad?

4. Were they confused by anything in the ad?

5. Would the ad persuade them to use your services the next time they buy or sell a home?

Use the information from the survey to make any needed changes in your advertising program. But a survey such as this one could only be conducted if you've been advertising over a period of months. If you've placed one ad, you don't have a track record to measure.

While some classified property ads can serve institutional purposes (getting your name out to the community), have you thought much about getting your name established with the sales associates you hope to hire and keep?

Salespeople are attracted to companies that are strong in marketing. If they notice your ads or see pictures of your associates in display

What Do Sales Associates Think?

ads, they will begin to see your company as one that will support them in their efforts to list and sell homes.

Just as a seller might question your advertising program during a listing presentation, a prospective sales associate will probably ask what kind of advertising the company does. You may not be able to measure how many of your salespeople have come to your firm or are staying with your company based on its advertising, but tell them that you're eliminating your ad budget and see how many you have left.

Are Your Ads Getting Listings?

Advertising is often used as a listing tool. If sellers think that advertising sells houses, they're going to list their property with the company that will advertise it the most. If that's true, then part of judging your advertising effectiveness will be based on how many listings you get from your ads and how happy your sellers are with your ads.

If you display full-page block ads during your listing presentations and sellers become anxious to sign your listing agreements, then your ads are accomplishing a lot — more listings than you would have had without them! Even if your block ads haven't led to one property sale and the phone hasn't rung very much, your ads are effective. But you wouldn't be able to measure their results by sales.

As you can see, evaluating your real estate advertising is an inexact science to say the least.

There are many reasons to advertise: to increase your business and profit, to get listings, to satisfy listings, to sell listings, to support and satisfy your salespeople and just for your own ego. Decide on your objective for each ad and then see if you've met your objective after the ad runs.

Direct-mail marketers frequently test their messages and their media and measure response from each. You will need to test and evaluate your ads as well. Test your publications by trying them over a period of a few months. If you see an increase in business, is it directly related to your advertising or other market factors? If you see a decrease, ask yourself the same question.

Don't be too harsh in judging the effectiveness of your advertising. Above all remember advertising doesn't sell, only you can do that.

Glossary I.
Real Estate Adjectives

The ad writer's "poetic license" allows for the free use of adjectives. However, using just the right word can make the difference between an ad that demands a phone call and one that hardly gets noticed.

For example, is the home you're writing about for the "discriminating" buyer or for the "distinguished" homeowner? You'll want to use these terms accurately, although some adjectives have very close meanings and are interchangeable. But make sure that any word you use will be readily understood by your audience. If you don't know the meaning of a word that you're using in an ad, chances are your readers won't either, so don't use it. You're trying to communicate with your reader, not impress him.

Following is a list of adjectives along with their meanings to help you avoid using the same tired descriptions over and over again and to make your listing classifieds come alive

— A —

ACCESSIBLE: Handy to, easy to reach, as in — Easily accessible to schools, churches and shopping....

ACCLAIMED: Praised by all who inspect, as in — Acclaimed by all to be the best home in this section....

ADVANCED: Better than ordinary construction, most modern, as in — Advanced design puts you years ahead....

APPEALING: Becoming, pleasant to look at, as in — Appealing to the pocketbook as well as the eye....

ARISTOCRATIC: Distinguished, as in — Aristocratic-looking from any angle....

ARTISTRY: Exacting workmanship, as in — The artistry in this home is quickly recognized....

AUTHENTIC: Genuine, not patterned after another, as in — An authentic Georgian colonial home....

— B —

BEWITCHING: Tempting, inviting, as in — This home is bewitching to all who stop to admire it....

BRILLIANT: Outshining all others, as in — The brilliant flowers and shrubs set this house apart....

— C —

CAPTIVATING: Desirable, wanted, as in — With a captivating, enclosed front porch....

CHARMING: Fascinating, alluring, captivating, captures your attention, as in — You will be amazed by the charming setting of this fine home....

CHERISHED: Popular, in demand, as in — A neighborhood that is cherished by every family....

CHIC: Stylish and smart, as in — The chic entrance will meet with approval....

CLASSIC: Not faddish, architecturally supreme, as in — Strictly a classic home in a classy neighborhood....

COMMENDABLE: Deserving of praise, as in — A commendable brick home highly recommended....

CONTRASTING: To show differences by comparison, as in — You will watch the garden change with its contrasting colors....

CONVINCING: Proof of value, as in — A value so convincing you will want the chance to buy as soon as you see it....

COZY: Snug, comfortable, as in — The cozy den is perfect for intimate quiet time....

— D —

DELICATE: Fragile, frail, as in — The delicate shades of the painted walls will please you....

DELIGHTFUL: Clean, healthy, happy, as in — A delightful neighborhood for children....

DIGNIFIED: Looked up to, expensive, as in — The dignified furnishings enhance the house....

DISCRIMINATING: Exacting, better than the majority, as in — Discriminating buyers will stop looking after seeing this....

DISTINCTIVE: Strong, outstanding, as in — A home distinctively modern in every way....

DISTINGUISHED: Prominent, pointed out, as in — Distinguished among higher-priced properties....

DOMINATING: Commanding, head and shoulders above competition, as in — The massive fireplace is dominating the living room....

DRAMATIC: Picturesque, awesome, as in — With a dramatic setting that is spellbinding....

— E —

ELABORATE: Detailed, ornate, as in — The elaborate landscape design includes flowers, grasses, trees and ornamental shrubs....

ELECTRIFYING: Thrilling, exciting, as in — This home has electrifying entertainment possibilities....

ELEGANT: Tasteful richness, refined gracefulness, as in — The elegant chandelier will enhance your dining room....

ELITE: Choice, best, upper class, as in — An elite neighborhood....

EMINENT: Best you can buy, as in — An eminent home for professionals....

ENCHANTING: Fascinating, charming, as in — A backyard of enchanting beauty....

ENDEARING: Lovely, captivating, as in — Endearing as your childhood days, this home....

ENDORSED: Recommended, approved, as in — With a heating system endorsed by Good Housekeeping....

ENDOWED: Enriched with appointments, as in — Endowed with built-in features you've always wanted....

ENDURING: Lasting, permanent, as in — With an enduring tile roof that will last a lifetime....

ENGAGING: Draw attention to, attractive, as in — With an engaging front door that welcomes your guests....

ENHANCED: Improved, better than original, as in — The kitchen lighting has been enhanced with a skylight....

ENTICING: Alluring, tempting, as in — The enticing master suite invites total relaxation from everyday worries....

EXQUISITE: Surpassing all others in quality, as in — The interior decorating in this home is exquisite....

EXTRAORDINARY: Above the ordinary, unusual, as in — You'll love the extraordinary pool and spa area....

EXTRAVAGANT: Excessive, exorbitant, as in — The extravagant window treatments include shades, blinds and custom draperies....

— F —

FASCINATING: Magnetic, gorgeous, as in — From every angle you'll find this home a fascinating one....

FASHIONABLE: Current trends in decorating, style, as in — Fashionable wallpaper decorates every room....

FLAWLESS: Without mistakes, perfect, as in — Examine the flawless condition....

FUTURISTIC: With something more than modern design and appointments, as in — You'll be up-to-date for many years with this futuristic home....

— G —

GALORE: Plenty of, an abundance, as in — Closets galore....

GAY: Bright, cheerful, as in — Gay colors in the children's bedrooms....

GENUINE: True, authentic, as in — Genuine hardwood floors throughout....

GLEAMING: Illuminating, bright, as in — With a gleaming all-tile bath....

GLISTENING: Sparkling, shining, as in — Built entirely of glistening white brick....

GLOWING: Warm coloring, exciting, as in — A home glowing with warmth and comfort....

GRACEFUL: Elegant, beauty in construction, as in — Graceful pines adorn the entrance to this country home....

GRATIFYING: Favorable, pleasurable, as in — The price is gratifying to the most conservative buyer....

— H —

HARMONIOUS: Blends well, in balance, as in — You'll like the harmonious decorating of all the rooms....

— I —

IMPECCABLE: Faultless, unblemished, as in — An impeccable interior with mint-condition appliances....

IMPOSING: Impressive, regal, as in — The imposing columns of this home welcome your guests....

IMPRESSIVE: Producing a vivid impression, as in — You'll find the tall trees in this neighborhood quite impressive....

INGENIOUS: Clever, shrewd, as in — This home has an ingenious floor plan that grows with the family....

IMMACULATE: Clean, spotless, as in — This immaculate home is ready to move into....

INSPIRING: Stimulating, exciting, as in — With an inspiring home office, ready for your work to begin....

INVITING: Beckoning, tempting, as in — An inviting library is off the formal living room....

— L —

LAVISH: Produced in abundance, as in — This home is perfect for the lavish lifestyle.....

LUSTROUS: Shining, radiant, brilliant, as in — The bathroom countertops are lustrous marble....

LUXURIOUS: Costly comfort in abundance, as in — Luxurious carpet and draperies come with this home....

— M —

MASSIVE: Big, bulky, as in — Enough room for your massive furnishings....

MATCHLESS: Without equal, none like it, as in — Of matchless design and architecture....

METICULOUS: Perfect in every detail, as in — The meticulous gardens you'll be proud to show off....

MODEST: Not elaborate or showy, as in — This modest home has the features you need at a modest price....

— N —

NOTEWORTHY: Remarkable, worthy of note, as in — It is noteworthy that this home was featured in the spring parade of homes....

NOVEL: New or unusual, as in — This home has a novel kitchen, especially designed for modern convenience....

— O —

ORNATE: Elaborately decorated, as in — The ornate wood moldings decorate each room....

— P —

PACE-SETTING: The leader, far ahead, as in — A pace-setting home in an upscale neighborhood....

PAINSTAKING: Took pains in creating so perfection could be achieved, as in — Craftsmen used painstaking dedication to create the kitchen....

PALATIAL: Like a mansion, estate, as in — You'll feel like royalty in the palatial grounds....

PARAMOUNT: Ranking among the best, supreme, as in — This home is paramount in every respect....

PICTURESQUE: Pretty as a picture, as in — The picturesque setting has no equal in this area....

PLUSH: Luxurious, rich, as in — The plush carpets cushion each footstep....

PRECIOUS: Of great value, desirable, as in — Nothing more precious than a home of your own....

PRUDENT: Sensible, safe, as in — A prudent investment decision....

— R —

RADIANT: Glowing, lustrous, brilliant, as in — Fireplace provides radiant glow....

REFINED: Cultured, aristocratic, as in — A refined neighborhood....

REFRESHING: Different, change of pace from the expected, as in — A refreshing floor plan with a bonus room....

REGAL: Noble, stately, as in — This home offers regal splendor....

— S —

SATISFYING: Pleasing, comfortable, as in — At a price and terms quite satisfying to any buyer....

SENSIBLE: Reasonable, intelligent, as in — You'll like the sensible features in this modest home....

SERENE: Still, calm, as in — You'll enjoy the serene comfort of the wooded setting....

SOPHISTICATED: Intellectually appealing, as in — For the most sophisticated investor....

SPARKLING: Glistening, gleaming, as in — A sparkling rushing stream crosses the property....

SPECTACULAR: Showing lavish improvements, as in — This spectacular home has every imaginable upgrade....

SPLENDID: Gorgeous, excellent, as in — A splendid location for this fine redwood shake home....

STUNNING: Strikingly beautiful, as in — Stunning custom-made built-in bookcases....

SUBSTANTIAL: Sturdy, massive, as in — The house rests on a substantial foundation....

SUPERB: Highest quality, gorgeous, as in — Truly superb landscaping design....

SURPASSING: Better than others, as in — Surpassing all other homes in this neighborhood....

— T —

TANTALIZING: Tempting, desirous, as in — A tantalizing swimming pool for hot summer days....

TEMPTING: Enticing, alluring, as in — A home so tempting that you'll want to move right in....

TRADITIONAL: Trend from years ago, historical value, as in — A huge dining room for celebrating traditional family gatherings....

TRANQUIL: Quiet, peaceful, as in — A tranquil pond encourages waterfowl to call it home....

TREASURE: Precious possession, great worth, as in — This home is a treasure you'll always cherish....

— U —

ULTIMATE: Utmost, absolute, supreme, as in — The ultimate in fine living....

UNIQUE: Only one of its kind, as in — The unique panoramic view....

UNRIVALED: Without a challenge, supreme, as in — An unrivaled home on a beautiful tree-lined street....

UNSURPASSED: Cannot be duplicated, uppermost, nothing better, as in — Unsurpassed condition....

— V —

VAST: Immense, extensive, as in — The vast improvements on this old home make it like new again....

VIBRANT: Thrilling, full of life, as in — In a community vibrant with neighbors who truly become friends....

Glossary II.
Advertising, Printing and Newspaper Terms

— A —

AGATE LINE: Measurement of vertical area roughly equal to 5.5 points. Chiefly used in billing vertical advertising space: 14 agate lines to the column inch.

— B —

BLEED: Extending printed image (usually photo) to the trim edge of the page.

BODY TYPE: Type used for the main text of the ad.

BOLD FACE: Letter of normal form and width but with heavier strokes.

— C —

CAMERA-READY: Any copy and design elements in finished form, ready for the printer to photograph or ready for the newspaper to "shoot." Used frequently in reference to ads supplied by the client that have no need for further typesetting or layout work.

CAPTION: Line or two of explanatory copy — usually under or above an illustration. Also called CUTLINE.

CLASSIFIED AD: Ad set in body type with little or no display type and grouped by subjects. Also called WANT AD or LINE AD.

COLUMN INCH: Area one inch deep and one column wide, used for measuring newspaper ads.

COMPOSITION: The setting and arranging of type.

CO-OP ADVERTISING: Ads cooperatively paid for by a local merchant and national sponsor or manufacturer, or ads paid for by more than one company.

COPY: All original material to be converted to type.

COPY EDIT: To correct written material for errors in style, grammar, content, etc.

COPY FIT: To determine mathematically the area a given amount of copy will occupy as type.

CROP MARKS: Indications on photo or artwork, showing which portions of the material are to be used.

— D —

DISPLAY AD: Advertising that uses larger than body type and is set off from the text of the newspaper by rules, white space or other devices such as borders.

DISPLAY TYPE: Type that has a larger size and different style than text type.

DOUBLE TRUCK: Ad using center spread of newspaper, designed to make use of gutters between pages.

DUMMY: A drawn plan of the layout of the newspaper page, used before final camera-ready material is prepared.

— E —

EDITORIAL: All material in the newspaper that is not advertising.

— F —

FACE: Style of type.

FLOP: To flip a photo over for layout purposes.

FLUSH LEFT: Type set so lines align at left margin.

FLUSH RIGHT: Type set so lines align at right margin.

FOUR-COLOR PROCESS: Reproduction in full color that adds black ink to the process primary colors of yellow, magenta and cyan.

— G —

GALLEY PROOF: Proof of type as it comes off the typesetting machine. One long single column before it is cut and pasted on the page in columns.

GLOSS PRINT: A photo printed on shiny paper, the preferred kind for newspaper reproduction.

GUTTER: Margins between facing pages.

— H —

HAIRLINE: Thinnest rule used in newspapers. Divides ads from editorial contents on the page.

HALFTONE: Continuous tone copy reproduced by means of photographing the image through a screen, breaking it up into a pattern of dots or lines that can then be printed. Halftone screens for offset-printed newspapers usually contain 85 lines to the inch.

HEAD or **HEADLINE:** Display type placed over body type to serve as attention getter for the ad.

— I —

INSERT: Separately printed material or newspaper section that must be inserted, usually manually, into the regular edition.

INSERTION: Your order for your ad with the newspaper.

ITALIC: Typeface that slants to the right.

— J —

JUSTIFIED COPY: Type set so that the left and right margins are straight with no ragged edge on either the left or right margin.

— K —

KILL: Cancel.

— L —

LAYOUT SHEET: Sheet printed with guiding rules in nonreproducible ink (usually blue), used as a base for your ad to be pasted on.

LEADING: Spacing between lines of type. Pronounced "ledding."

LETTER-SPACING: Additional spacing between letters in a typeset word.

LINE ART: Artwork that appears in simple masses of black and white, as opposed to continuous tone (with shades of gray).

LOWER CASE: Small letters of the alphabet.

— M —

MECHANICAL: Camera-ready piece including type and artwork.

— N —

NEWSPRINT: The type of paper used to print newspapers.

— P —

PASTEUP: The process of arranging and affixing to a mechanical, pieces of type and art in preparation for printing.

PHOTOTYPESETTING: Method of type composition in which images are placed photographically on film or paper.

PICA: Unit of printer's measurement, approximately one-sixth of an inch.

PICKUP: An ad that doesn't need to be reset.

POINT: Printer's unit of measurement, approximately 1/72 inch.

PRESS RELEASE: Publicity copy submitted to a newspaper as a means of self-promotion.

PROPORTIONAL SCALE: A circular slide rule used in figuring percentages of enlargement and reduction for photos.

PYRAMID: The pattern for arranging ads as a triangle on facing pages.

— R —

RAGGED LEFT: Unjustified type, arranged so that the left margin is not aligned.

RAGGED RIGHT: Unjustified type, arranged so that the right margin is not aligned.

RATE HOLDER: Ad that is published to fulfill a contract requirement for a minimum number of lines or inches.

REGISTRATION: Two or more printing images aligned exactly on top of each other.

REVERSE: Printed area with black background on which type appears in white (when using black ink).

R.O.P: Acronym for Run of Paper position, rather than in the classified section.

— S —

SANS SERIF: Type style which lacks small finishing strokes at the end of main strokes of each letter.

SCREEN: Device used to convert continuous tone art to halftone by means of breaking it into dots of black or white. Can be used as background for type in an ad.

SERIF: Small finishing stroke at the end of main stroke of type.

SIGNATURE: Name, address and phone number of the advertiser usually placed in prominent area of ad or at close of classified ad.

STAT: Photostatic copy of ad closely resembling the way it will reproduce in the newspaper.

SUBHEAD: Short line of display type used under the main headline for the ad or a short line of centered text type, usually in bold face, used to break up long columns of body type.

— T —

TEAR SHEET: A page torn out of the printed publication, usually used as a proof to an advertiser that his ad has appeared.

TYPEFACE or TYPE STYLE: A family of type having a particular design, designated by names such as Bodoni, Triumvirate or Souvenir.

TYPO: Error made in typesetting.

— U —

UPPER CASE: Capital letters of the alphabet.

— V —

VELOX: Photoprint with image in halftone dot pattern rather than in continuous tones.

— W —

WHITE SPACE: The area in an ad that contains no type or art.

Appendix A.
Don't Write One Without It — The Headline

Headlines are your attention-getters. Avoid writing any ad without a headline. But writing a great headline is sometimes more difficult than writing the body copy.

While all listings have different features and benefits, the appeal, type of buyer and reason the property is attractive is the same for many homes.

Use these suggested ad headlines to attract specific buyers' attention. Just determine the home's appeal, then look for the heading for that category and select the appropriate headline. Most of these heads are geared to classified ad formats, but they can also be adapted for a display listing ad.

The next time you're stumped coming up

with an appealing headline, turn to this section.
The following headlines for your listings are
based on their appeal — to a large family, an
investor, the executive or the bargain hunter.

For Your Big Family

Oversized Home

This One's for the Kids

For Your Choosy Family

Bedrooms Galore

Kids Wanted!

Kids' Place

A Family Delight

The Smart Family Home

Family Pleaser

Great Neighborhood for Kids

Close to Schools

Family Sized and Styled

Make Your Family Happy

Families

Fits Your Family

Are You the Lucky Family?

For Family Fun

Does Your Family Come First?

For Your Growing Family

Have You Outgrown Your Home?

Bargain Hunters, Starters or Fixers

Waiting for a Bargain? Here It Is.

This Home's a Bargain

Thrifty Thinking

More for Your Money

What Value!

What a Buy!

Trim Price

Right in Your Budget

This Will Balance Your Budget

Perfect for the First-time Buyer

Looking for That First Home? Here It Is.

Great Starter Home

You Can Afford This Home

Lots of Room at a Low Price

Affordable

You Can Buy This Home

Turn from Renter to Happy Homeowner

Rent No More

Interested in a Low Down Payment?

The Price Breaker

Motivated Seller

Try Any Offer

Low Price

Best Buy

Unbelievable House at a Believable Price

Priced Below Market

Below Appraised Value

Super Price

Looking for Yesterday's Prices
   on Today's Homes?

Calling All Offers

Priced Right for You

Priced for Quick Sale

Won't Last at This Price

If Price Is Important

Down to Your Price

Low, Low Price

No Home on the Market Matches This Value

Nice Home, Nicer Price

A Fixer and a Saver

You Fix, You Save

Fun to Fix

Bring Your TLC

Fixer-Upper

Handyman Special

Great Location, Just Needs Work

Lots of Work and Lots of Possibility

Sound, But Neglected

You Increase the Value

Great Potential, Great Price

Some Creative Rehab Wanted

All It Needs Is Work, Not a Lot of Money

Estate Sale

Foreclosure

Lender Now Owns

Your Dream Home

Magnificent Luxury

A Gracious Home for You

You're Not Dreaming

Once in a Lifetime

Executive or Luxury Home

No Exaggerating

Perfection

Everything You're Looking For

Your Own Shangri-la

The World of Luxury Living

High Style

Want the Best?

End of the Rainbow

You've Hit the Jackpot

Your Palace Awaits

For the Discriminating Buyer

Dream No More

Who Says Dreams Don't Come True?

For Fine Living

Executive Home

Executive Entertaining Here

This Home's the Talk of the Town

264

Peak of Perfection

You'll Be Envied

A Home to Match Your Successful Lifestyle

For a Better Way of Life

Superb

A Rare Find

Exceptional

Stunning

Life at the Top

Spectacular in Every Way

Dramatic

Mint Estate

Incredible Beauty

Everything You Ever Wanted

Match Your Success

Lots of Flair

You Have Arrived

The Ultimate

Accent on Elegance

Pride of Ownership

Prestigious Location

You Won't Compromise Here

Reward Your Success

Investors

Investor's Dream

Great Investment Opportunity

Positive Cash Flow Here

Sound Condition and Ready to Rent

You Be the Landlord

Attention Investors

Below Appraisal

Looking for the Right Profit Opportunity?

Looking for Steady Income?

This One's a Money Maker

Very Profitable for You

Already Leased

You Can Increase Rents

Tax Benefits from a Great Investment

Good Rental Location

Investor Priced

For the First-time Real Estate Investor

For the Future-minded Investor

A Blue Chip Investment

Income Shelter, Plus Income Maker

Price and Terms Are Right

Add to Your Income

Let's Make a Deal

Appendix B.
Add Sales Power With Descriptive Body Copy

Once you've grabbed your readers' attention with your headline, you'll need to keep them motivated by explaining the property's benefits in the body copy. Before the reader becomes your next "up call," this part of the ad must develop the readers' interest in the property and reinforce the appeal made in the headline.

In a display ad, these benefits might be bulleted to get quick attention from the reader. In a classified, your ad must sound more emotionally appealing than all the others on the page.

Following are ideas to build descriptive body copy. These phrases are listed under the rooms or other prominent features of the home. Just check the headings for the rooms or features that you have decided to include and use one of the phrases that best describes the property. Or use these ideas to get your own creative thinking started.

The final heading includes closing phrases to urge your reader to action — namely calling you and setting an appointment.

So complete and well planned

An inspiration to any cook

Counter space galore

All built-ins included

Step-saving, modern kitchen

A pleasure to cook in

You'll be twice the cook in half the time

A kitchen the whole family will use

Expertly planned

Efficient

Easy-care

Built-in new microwave for quick snacks and meals

Kitchen

Family-size kitchen

Beauty, comfort and convenience

Extra storage and cabinets

Meal-size kitchen

With convenient breakfast bar for hurried meals

Breakfast room has full garden view

New appliances

Custom cabinetry

Gourmet kitchen

Designer kitchen

Functional work island

Completely modern

Open to family room for watching the little ones

Bright and airy

Cheerful wallpaper

Breakfast nook for casual, comfy meals

Country kitchen

Eat-in kitchen

Efficient galley

Step-saver

Spacious, but intimate dining for two to twenty

Enjoy sophisticated entertaining

Ideal for your most formal affair

Perfect for large family get-togethers

Adds a note of elegance to everyday dining

Party-perfect dining room

Banquet sized

Casual and contemporary

Old-fashioned warmth

A room you'll be proud to serve in

Convenient to kitchen and living room for easy
entertaining

Dining Room

Family Room

The focal point for fun family entertaining

Relaxing and recreational

Family headquarters

Great for kids' games and activities

Informal center for family hobbies

Spacious and separate from bedrooms

Could be a fitness center or game room

Can be library or cozy den

You'll spend all your time in this room

Family room/media room — great for stereo and large screen TV

Family room is perfect for teenage get-aways

Plenty of built-ins

A fireplace that's a conversation piece

Favorite spot for the family

Family-sized family room

Paneled and rustic

Wallpapered and contemporary

Blends with any decor

Family room that will become the meeting room
for kids' activities

Secluded bedroom wing

Separate master bedroom wing

Luxurious master suite

Lavish master bedroom with private bath

Master suite is on a level of its own

Nursery already here

Great for teens and private for homework

Lots of built-ins and bookshelves

Elegance carried throughout the bedrooms

Plenty of space for the largest bedroom set

Breezy bedrooms

Room for doubles in these bedrooms

King-sized bedrooms, for king size beds

Bed-rooms

Room for everything bedrooms

Looking for that extra guest bedroom?

Extra bedrooms for sewing, music, study or office

Living Room

Elegant

For formal entertaining

Charming and warm

Dramatic, sunken

Complements any furnishings or style

Cathedral ceiling adds class

You'll be proud to entertain here

Casual enough for family living

Here's the space you've been looking for

Roomy

Entertainment-sized

The room to show off your furnishings and collectibles

Great gathering spot

Sumptuous private master bath

Baths

Master bath with dressing room

Spa-jetted bathtub for relaxing

Luxurious master bath with skylights and atrium

Double basin vanities for busy mornings

Custom baths with quality features

Updated baths that sparkle with color and light

Enough baths for family and guests

Easy to maintain ceramic tile walls and counters

You'll be proud to show your guests the bright guest bath

Having overnight guests? Plenty of extra baths

Convenient shower stall with new clear glass doors

Finished interior makes garage pleasant to work in

Garage

Extra storage room with built-in shelves in garage

Big enough for your full-size cars and more

Have tools, toys and tinkering to do? Here's the place

Clutter vanishes with all the garage built-ins

Garage can easily be converted to extra living space. Walls and ceiling already in

Already has electric garage door opener for convenience

Separate heating system in garage for year-round workshop

Lot

Easy maintenance yard

Low maintenance landscaping

Wooded and shaded lot for low energy bills in summer

Completely private yard

Secluded lot for family entertaining

Beautiful rock garden in backyard

Have your own private pond

Listen to the babbling of the creek nearby

Professionally landscaped, everything's been done for you to enjoy

On automatic sprinklers for easy maintenance

Backs up to open space with lots of trees, birds and nature

Small and well-planned yard

Picture perfect yard with trees for shade and flowers for color

Relaxing patio for outdoor entertaining

Rustic wood deck for summer barbecues

Overlooks scenic area with man-made lake

Room to play

Bring your swingset and backyard barbecue

Park-like setting

Your own private park

Large enough for pool or tennis court

Manicured lawn

Location

View of mountains, back country or water

Three blocks to public transportation

Backs up to park

A prestigious address

Exclusive address

You have arrived

Move up to the best location

Near churches

Near shopping

Near public and private schools

You can walk to work

On a private street

On a cul-de-sac for safety and privacy

Golf course community

Bike to the beach

In a choice location

Great family neighborhood

Bedroom community

Near commuter bus

Near new shopping mall

Near all major attractions

Find everything you need nearby

Quiet street

Quiet residential area

Privacy plus prestige

An area of estate homes

Established community of fine homes

New area — come and meet the neighbors

Raised hearth fireplace for cozy family get-togethers

Automatic gas starter for easy entertaining

Bring the logs for a real wood-burning fire

**Fire-
places,
Sky-
lights,
Details**

Heat efficient fireplace, you'll use and enjoy

Impressive, floor-to-ceiling fireplace

Rustic brick blends with any decor

Carved wooden mantle for elegant display

Natural stone makes an unusual statement

The elegance of marble, accents the hearth

Old fashioned warmth combined with modern heat efficiency

Gas logs make having a fire an everyday occasion

Skylights flood natural light into the home

Capture afternoon sunlight with practical skylights

Skylight directs lighting into your work area

Bring morning sun into your room with the skylight

Loaded with extras

Completely remodeled and modern

Dramatic vaulted ceilings

Custom moldings that add distinction

Walk out onto your own private patio through elegant French doors

Upgraded storm doors and windows that conserve heat in winter

Custom window treatments that match any decor

Unusual wood plank ceiling

Upgraded carpeting in neutral, light tone

Easy-care floor coverings

Award-winning architecture

Functional floor plan

Extra storage shelves built-in to every closet

Oversized walk-in closets in the bedrooms

Mirrored closet doors for that touch of elegance

Fully insulated for energy savings

Year-round comfort — completely air conditioned

Well designed pool, practically cares for itself

The kids will love the sparkling pool

Family-size pool for a fun filled summer

Low cost family entertainment — your own heated and filtered pool

Separate fenced-in pool area

Closing Phrases

Don't miss seeing this home today.

Happy living starts here.

Don't put off seeing this home.

Call today!

If you've been waiting for an exceptional value, here it is!

Be the first to see this home.

Here's the home for you.

See it today!

Stop house hunting and call now.

Nothing compares in price and value.

Stop by the open house or call for a private showing.

Don't be disappointed, don't delay, call today!

Don't miss seeing this home before you buy.

Move in for the holidays.

Start packing!

Call the movers.

See this great buy.

There's more. Call us to find out.

See this home and you'll make an offer.

All offers considered.

Stop your house hunting!

Best value in today's market.

You can't match this value and price.

It may be gone tomorrow.

We'll show you how easy it is to afford.

Appendix C.
Who Are Your Buyers? What Are They Looking For?

Before you start advertising properties or determining the market for a listing, wouldn't it be helpful to know just what buyers are looking for in their next home?

If price is the main consideration, then you know to mention it in the headline for your ad. If most buyers are looking for top school systems, you can stop writing about cozy fireplaces and start emphasizing excellent education. This type of information is invaluable.

Some newspapers survey their readers on their attitudes toward products and then share this information with advertisers. Ask your ad sales representative if such surveys have been done in your area. If not, you may be interested in learning the attitudes of buyers in the tri-state *New York Times* area.

In its "1986 Real Estate Perspectives" report, marketing researchers from the *Times* interviewed first-time and trade-up buyers who said they were likely to buy a home within two years.

Following are some of the statistics you may find helpful in planning your advertising for this area. You can, of course, also adapt the findings to your own area advertising.

51 percent of the prospective buyers

Median age: 32

Married: 54 percent

Both spouses working full-time: 34 percent

Attended college or have degrees: 71 percent

Household income less than $35,000: 52 percent

No children: 62 percent

Consider real estate to be a better investment than stocks, bonds, gold or antiques: 66 percent

Desire a single-family home: 57 percent

Desire a "good price" on a home: 24 percent

First-time Buyers

Desire a specific neighborhood: 25 percent

Desire a bigger home: 5 percent

Desire a certain atmosphere or facilities:
5 percent

Desire certain schools: less than 1 percent

Active Buyers

(Bought a home within the last five years and say they are likely to buy another in next two years)

19 percent of the prospective buyers

Median age: 35.4

Married: 82 percent

Both spouses working full-time: 41 percent

Attended college or have degrees: 82 percent

Household income over $50,000: 53 percent

No children: 45 percent

Consider real estate to be a better investment than stocks, bonds, gold or antiques:
76 percent

Desire a single-family home: 77 percent

Desire a "good price" on home: 17 percent

Desire a certain neighborhood: 40 percent

Desire a bigger home: 9 percent

Desire a certain atmosphere or facilities:
   3 percent

Desire certain schools: 1 percent

(Bought a home more than five years ago and say they are likely to buy another in the next two years)

Veteran Buyers

30 percent of the prospective buyers

Median age: 41

Married: 69 percent

Both spouses working full-time: 25 percent

Attended college or have degrees: 66 percent

Household income over $50,000: 44 percent

No children: 50 percent

Desire a single-family home: 63 percent

Desire a "good price" on a home: 10 percent

Desire a certain neighborhood: 28 percent

Desire a bigger home: 10 percent

Desire certain atmosphere or facilities:
5 percent

Desire certain schools: less than 1 percent

Appendix D.
How Do Real Estate Buyers and Sellers Use the Media?

From research conducted in 1984, the *Minneapolis Star and Tribune* published a report called "The New Metropolitan Marketplace." This study analyzed changes in the residential market in the Minneapolis metropolitan area, including data on how buyers and sellers used the media.

The introduction states: "We believe that, armed with this market material, you can make better use of your advertising dollar, and best of all, increase your sales."

Following are some of the data that are intended to help real estate professionals.

Are more singles becoming homeowners?

In 1978, 17 percent of all home buyers were

single. By 1983, that figure had risen to 32 percent as more individuals and unrelated joint purchasers invested in homes.

Do buyers know where they want to live?

Nearly three out of four buyers (72 percent) opted for an existing (rather than new) home. Home buyers also know where they want to live: 81 percent said they preferred an area and 92 percent actually bought in the neighborhood they wanted.

What are the reasons for buying?

— 29 percent want a larger house
— 22 percent want to own a house
— 16 percent are interested in tax/investment advantages
— 15 percent have experienced a job or school transfer
— 6 percent want to change the area they live in
— 4 percent need less room

What are the reasons for selling?

— 25 percent want a larger house
— 24 percent have experienced a job or school transfer
— 21 percent want a smaller house
— 12 percent want to live in a different area
— 4 percent are interested in tax/investment advantages

What advertising do home buyers find helpful?

— 70 percent said the Sunday *Star* and *Tribune*
— 34 percent said the Saturday *Star* and *Tribune*
— 33 percent said the *St. Paul* Sunday
— 28 percent said the daily *Star* and *Tribune*
— 27 percent said *Homes for Sale* magazines
— 16 percent said the daily *St. Paul*
— 15 percent said the Saturday *St. Paul*
— 5 percent said television
— 4 percent said radio

What days do home buyers look at real estate ads?

— 59 percent said Sunday
— 34 percent said Saturday
— 26 percent said weekdays
— 13 percent said no particular day
— 11 percent said everyday

Appendix E.
Buyer/Seller Survey

'Up calls" are a significant way of tracking ad response. But the number of actual sales and listings that result from ads are even more important to track. Sometimes, sales associates don't note the motivating factor behind a recent sale no matter how many forms for this are provided and used in the office.

The following postage-paid survey card can be sent directly to the client after the sale has closed to increase the tracking of what contributed to the sale.

BUYER/SELLER SURVEY

Thank you for letting us handle your recent real estate transaction. In order for us to better serve you and other clients in the future, we would appreciate your answers to the following brief questions. Thanks for your time.

1. How did you hear of our company? Do you recall why you specifically used our services?

____ knew the sales associate
____ was referred to the sales associate by a friend
____ open house
____ yard sign
____ advertisement
____ name of publication _____

____ community event _____

____ other _____

2. Were you satisfied with our service?

3. Would you recommend our company to an acquaintance?

4. Do you know of anyone now who is interested in buying or selling a home in our community? Please print their name below.

5. Comments or suggestions:

_____

_____

Your name: _____

Address: _____

Telephone: _____

Index